Plato, George Henry Wells

The Euthyphro of Plato

With Introduction and Notes

Plato, George Henry Wells

The Euthyphro of Plato
With Introduction and Notes

ISBN/EAN: 9783337008765

Printed in Europe, USA, Canada, Australia, Japan

Cover: Foto ©Thomas Meinert / pixelio.de

More available books at **www.hansebooks.com**

THE EUTHYPHRO

OF

PLATO

WITH

AN INTRODUCTION AND NOTES

BY

GEORGE HENRY WELLS, B.A.

Scholar of St. John's College Oxford, and Assistant Master at Bradfield College.

LONDON :

GEORGE BELL AND SONS,

YORK STREET, COVENT GARDEN

1881.

AD VENERABILEM ARCHIDIACONUM

JACOBUM AUGUSTUM HESSEY, D.C.L.,

PRECEPTOREM DILECTISSIMUM.

PREFACE.

THE value of the Euthyphro as a specimen of Platonic writing has been fully recognised by scholars; its greatest defect being, perhaps, its brevity; and it has seemed to the writer that, if well mastered, the Dialogue will serve as an excellent introduction to the larger and more advanced compositions of Plato.

The writer of these Notes thanks most sincerely those who have, by their countenance or recommendations, enabled him to give his work to the public; especially Rev. C. T. CRUTTWELL, Head Master of Bradfield College, Dr. HUCKIN, of Repton School, Dr. BAKER, of Merchant Taylors' School, Dr. GALLOP, of Christ's College, Finchley, and Rev. A. J. CHURCH, of Retford School. He is also much indebted to his colleague, A. D. GODLEY, Esq., for valuable assistance in revision of proofs.

BRADFIELD,
  December 1879.

CONTENTS.

THE EUTHYPHRO OF PLATO.

INTRODUCTION.

" In the *Meno*, Amytus had parted from Socrates with the threatening words, that ' in any city, and particularly in the city of Athens, it is easier to do men harm than to do them good :' and Socrates was anticipating another opportunity of talking with him. In the *Euthyphro*, Socrates is already awaiting his trial for impiety in the porch of the king Archon. But before the trial proceeds Plato would like to put the world on their trial, and convince them of ignorance in that very matter touching which Socrates is accused. An incident which may perhaps really have occurred in the family of Euthyphro, a learned Athenian diviner and soothsayer, furnishes the occasion of the discussion."

In these words Professor Jowett opens his introduction to the dialogue of the *Euthyphro*, one of the smaller but not less interesting dialogues which are concerned with the trial and condemnation of Socrates on a charge of impiety. To grasp the bearing of the dialogue, and to realise fully the circumstances of it, it will be well to glance shortly at the history of Greek religious thought, at the phenomenon of Socrates and his method of inquiry, and at the collision, as Plato gives it, between the Athenian philosopher and the Athenian Conservatives.

And first, with regard to the origin and progress of religious inquiry in Greece, we must look back to the mythical Greece of Achilles, of Theseus, and of Agamemnon, as a country where the king rules, the priests perform religious offices, and the people obey both, as a matter of course, and as an obedience to tradition. The kings and the priests rule because they have found power placed in their hands, and the people obey because it has never occurred to them to do otherwise, or to question the divine right of kings—

$$\text{οἴτε θέμιστας} \atop \text{πρὸς Διὸς εἰρύαται,[1]}$$

nor to dispute the propriety of religious observances. They were taught that the man who did his duty to his country and his country's gods was sure to prosper, that he would be θεοῖς φίλος, just as one who trespassed was θεοῖς ἐχθρὸς. Such was the religious attitude, uninquiring and restful.

By far the most important part of religion at this period was the observance of outward forms—forms which marked the worshipper as a true brother and member of the state under whose auspices they were performed ; just as in the subdivisions of the state—the φρατρίαι or *gentes*—there were solemn sacrifices offered at stated times when the presence of all heads of houses —φράτερες or clansmen—was required. In an early stage of civilisation such a mode of expressing confraternity was felt to be necessary, to prevent schism in the state and guarantee security by vows of mutual defence and good offices. This junction of the religious and clannish

---

[1] *Il.* 1, 239.

sentiment made the former more interesting and the latter more sacred. And such was religion in its civil or political aspect. But if we turn to the side of religion which respected the individual—the subjective side— what do we find? We find that the belief of which these outward forms and observances were the symbols, was—at any rate with respect to the gods—the secondary and the minor consideration. Belief, actively exercised, scarcely occurred to the worshipper of this period; and, if it did occur, had little importance attached to it.

Nor was it required as long as this unquestioning, obedient attitude was preserved towards religion. The prayers and sacrifices were regularly made; and, although certain gods might be less respected than others for their cowardice or lust, still such anthropomorphism made the religion easier of acceptance as a whole. If it had occurred to a Greek of this age we are considering to say, "These gods are nought," he would have been laughed at, more for his inaptness than his impiety. "At any rate," the reply would have been, "they are the gods to whom our fathers prayed, and they were prosperous upon the earth: why then should not we follow them? Let well alone." Such a question was not suited to that age : the mind was not in a stage to receive such a consideration as the existence or non-existence of the gods.

But the inherent activity of the Greek intellect soon began to move from this resting-place, stimulated probably by contact with the culture and science of Egypt. The birth of Thales, commonly known as the first Ionic philosopher, or physicist, an Ionian, is placed about 639 B.C. In him we see the beginning of a new stage of thought, viz. that of scientific inquiry. This inquiry took at first the direction of physics. Such a man as

Thales would have looked round upon the universe and said to himself, " What and whence is all this ?" And inquiries of this kind continued to be made with more or less assiduity down to the time we are specially considering and beyond. The question, then arises—" How did such inquiries affect popular beliefs and popular theology ?" To answer this question we must ask first— " Who was the embodiment of the old religion ? and what was the conception of Deity ?" And we shall find that the ultimate authority, the supreme being, of religious contemplation was Zeus, in effect a glorified man, not very remote from the popular conception of a Hercules or a Theseus. True, behind Zeus there sometimes peeped out a still more important authority—Fate, Dire Necessity ; but practically the religious horizon was bounded by the conception called Zeus. He was πατὴρ ἀνδρῶν τε θεῶν τε : and the Greeks said of themselves, Ἐκ Διὸς ἔσμεν. Now when men began to speculate, the authority of Zeus, like the authority of all other matters of traditional acceptance, came to be questioned. And other sources of all existence began to be looked for instead of the god Zeus, the only quality which was preserved from the conception of a god being that of unity. So for cloud-compelling Zeus one physicist substituted *water* as the origin of all things, and another *matter*, a third *air ;* again we have a higher ideal of *being*, and of *mind*, of *number*, and of *change.* Ζεὺς ὅστις ποτ' ἐστὶν,[1] exclaims the chorus of old Argive senators in the *Agamemnon* of Æschylus ;— " Zeus whoever he may be," implying an instability of belief in a personal God that seems marvellously out of place in Athens the home of gods—an instability exemplified in many other passages in the earliest writers.

[1] Æsch. *Ag.* 160.

If such speculations, on the origin of existence as affecting popular beliefs and traditions, had been confined to the chamber of the speculator, their result might have been considerably retarded but hardly suppressed. As it was, they were not concealed but given to the world. The men who speculated were generally prominent characters, being attached to the court and person of some tyrant or leading politician; and from such a position the propagation of their ideas was easy. But as long as these ideas were entertained and these inquiries were conducted under the protection and with the countenance of powerful patrons, the propagation was but limited. Such inquiries did not touch the bulk of the citizens, who were not amenable to the philosophers' influence, but were confined to the court of the tyrant or the clique of the minister. They were the relaxation of the learned, not the gospel for the ignorant. Such was the position occupied by the earlier philosophers.

Passing on next to that period when despotism was everywhere making room for democracy, we find philosophy in bad case; and, in this regard, democracy shows more tyrannical than tyranny. For what tyranny had countenanced or encouraged—viz. freedom of speculation—democracy, in its puristic care of the children of the state, would not hear of. Let us illustrate this change of bearing by an example. Anaxagoras, born c. B.C. 500, was an Ionian, settled at Athens, and the friend of Pericles. He had elaborated a system of philosophy in his mind which left him no interest in politics. This want of political taste was, as we know, a heinous fault in a Greek state. Even Solon, the equitable lawgiver, had forbidden citizens to "be of no side" in a political contest. although Solon knew well that political contests frequently were settled only by civil war. In conformity with these facts Anaxagoras was marked out as a man worthy of indictment; and notice what the indictment was. Not merely that he was guilty of impiety—that he had enthroned Νους as Lord and Father of all things in the stead of Zeus—but that he was guilty of sedition. He was accused of Medism, i.e. of Persian proclivities, when, as Maurice remarks, "probably the fact that there was such an empire as the Persian existing had escap d him." He was in consequence obliged to fly from Athens, and Pericles' reputation suffered a temporary eclipse from supposed complicity with the dangerous philosopher.

We have, then, in Greek thought at this time the onward moving and the retarding element. Let us examine them. The Greek word expressing sedition, or revolutionary tendencies, is νεωτερισμός; to be a seditious person is καινίζειν or νεωτερίζειν,, i.e. a promulgator of new things. This word, bearing as it usually does a bad sense, embodies at once the conservatism (implied in the condemnatory use of the word) and a more important trait of the Greek mind, wnich we may call the Inquisitive, the Radical, or the Destructive, in whichever light we may regard it. The person who uses the word νεωτερισμός disapproves of the νεωτεριστής, who is none the less a fact in Greek politics and Greek society. This latter trait was really the stronger, and became ultimately the pervading one in Greece; but the conservative element was strong also and died hard, numbering amongst its defenders such champions as Aristophanes. In a matter of life and death—for such was this struggle regarded at any rate by the Conservatives—it is not to be wondered at if the blows were not always well directed, or if they did not always hit the mark intended. Such a misdirected blow —to carry on the metaphor—was the prosecution of Socrates for impiety by Meletus, Anytus, and Lyco. These prosecutors were men striking in the dark : they could feel that Socrates was a prominent and an assailable figure, and so they struck, but scarcely knew why. Like Anaxagoras, Socrates was a philosopher; like him, also, Socrates was prosecuted for impiety. But before showing how this dialogue with Euthyphro springs out of the story of Socrates' indictment, we must pause to speak a few words about this unique and soul-stirring character, Socrates.

Socrates, son of Sophroniscus, was an Athenian citizen, born c. B.C. 468. He was of a constitution extraordinarily robust, and of an unprepossessing appearance. He had served with credit in military campaigns at Potidæa, Delium, and Amphipolis; and he had taken part in public trials and in legislation. In the latter department he had gained a character of strict impartiality with some, and of obstinacy with most of the Athenians, owing to his rigorous obedience to his principle. He was, in one word, a man of strong conviction —that is the keynote to his character; and perhaps we shall not err in saying that the strength of his convictions was never surpassed by that of any other man. He attributed this strength of his convictions to a supernatural, accompanying influence, which he called his δαιμόνιον, or spirit. What is conveyed exactly by this term is hard to say. Plato's account of it is as follows : that it was a φωνή, or monitorial voice, that it had been with him from a child, that it prevented him from taking part in politics, and that it never originated action, but only prevented particular acts. ἀεὶ ἀποτρέπει προτρέπει δὲ οὔποτε. Socrates himself

looked upon it as a direct spiritual deterrent, to guard
him from wrong acts which ignorance or rashness might
suggest, to the temporary subjection of his better judg-
ment.   The Christian will see in it a strong similarity
to the voice of conscience.   Dr. Riddell's note in his
edition of the *Apologia* gives a full account of the
passages bearing on the subject, and will be consulted
with advantage.   Socrates' psychological history was
given as follows by himself : he had a great desire for
wisdom and knowledge, in the search for which he
never rested.   But he found it so difficult of acquire-
ment that he was nearly in despair.   For in his search,
although he approached, as was natural, all kinds of
men with reputations for wisdom and for knowledge,
scientific and otherwise, he found that—to use his own
expression—they all of them knew nothing and yet
thought they did.   And this discovery, by the way,
confirmed his belief in the truth of the Delphic oracle,
from which he had learnt with surprise that he was
himself the wisest man on earth.   " For," he concluded,
"if all these would-be wise men say that they know
and know not, then I, who do not know, but confess
my ignorance, am in this respect wiser than them all."
A negative conclusion, and one eminently characteristic
of Socrates.   He then made it the business of his life
in the first place to convict men of their ignorance, and
in the second to supply as much positive knowledge as
could be educed from conversational intercourse between
himself, his followers and friends, and the Athenian
public.   He did not arrogate the title and position of
teacher in these conversations, or rather *conversaziones ;*
he was rather the director, who encouraged the conversation and pointed out who was on the right track,
and where error lay.   He met every man on equal

ground, presupposed no superior information in himself, but rather seemed to give others credit for it, and
endeavoured by a method of conversational argument,
as logical as the age permitted, to set in their true light
and reduce to their truest form, any statements that
might be hazarded by the speaker or might appear
in the course of the conversation. A favourite means
of bringing out the ignorance of a dogmatic conversa-
tionist was this affected ignorance of Socrates—his
εἰρωνεία, as it was called. By putting forward his
ignorance, he would lead the other speaker on to rash
assertions, the falsity of which could be easily demonstrated by a rigorous application of logic, thereby
confuting positions which might often have been held
by less aggressive advocates of their soundness. Another
point of importance in Socrates' method is his recog-
nition of the value of definition. "Define Piety," says
Socrates. The answer is, "Piety is doing as I am now
doing, viz. bringing a guilty man to justice." "No;
that is pious," replies Socrates; "a particular act of
piety, not piety itself." In this word-fencing, which
bears so conspicuous a part in the dialogues of Plato,
Socrates is not always strictly consistent : he is not
above using a little quibbling here and there to convict
a man of false statement, so long as he is convicted.[1]
And to finish our sketch of Socrates as the dialectician,
we must not omit a pleasant trait[2]—his repugnance to
the idea of taking money for his teaching ; nor his
humour ;[3] nor the unbounded patience with which he
brought out a conclusion or demonstrated an error. It
remains to say a word upon the outcome of Socrates'
practice of conversation in Athens. The immediate
outcome was the death of Socrates. And why? We

---

[1] *v. not. ad* c. xv.　　　[2] c. iii.　　　[3] ch. l.

have seen the age of inquiry succeeding the age of belief
and repose. We hear Athenian νεωτερίζοντες asking of
everything—" Why is this so ? What authority have
we for this statement, that institution ? " Socrates lived
in the very *mêlée* of such an age. Since the philosophers
and poets had first started the ball of inquiry, it had
been rolling with ever-increasing velocity, shaking and
overturning everything that could not offer a firm re-
sistance. Inquiry is a noble right of mankind, but,
like all rights, is liable to perversion. Such perversion
follows when the inquirers are unscrupulous, depraved,
or ignorant. Socrates represents the enlightened inquirer ; he was taken for the depraved one. Of this
latter type specimens abounded, who were guilty of the
moral iconoclasm, the excesses, the perversions of youth,
the stupid insubordination to constituted authority, of
which Socrates and his friends were accused, and for
which Socrates paid the penalty of death. To conclude :
we might not inaptly term the period of Socrates' accusation and death the Athenian Revolution ; for in the
mental history of mankind it was the culmination of
the greatest movement the world has ever seen. At
that time philosophy, literature, psychology, and
science were receiving a direction and an influence
the effect of which has by no means yet ceased to be
felt.

· Whatever doubts may have been thrown on the
authenticity of the *Euthyphro* as a genuine Platonic
dialogue can hardly fail to be dispelled on its perusal.
In its masterly delineation of character, its perspicacity
of style, its grasp of dialectic, and its elucidation of
truth by the confutation of error, it is worthy of a place

by the side of the best of Plato's dialogues, and although one of the shortest, it is one of the most typical. Here are the Socratic logic, the Socratic εἰρωνεία, the protest against the popular theology, the conception of unity in plurality, the antagonism against spurious knowledge, and the " conclusion where nothing is concluded "—all embraced in a short conversation of a few pages. The dialogue arises out of the prosecution of Socrates on a charge of impiety by Meletus, Anytus, and Lyco. In the words of Professor Jowett, quoted above, Plato would like to try the world for impiety before the world proceeds to try Socrates. And Plato takes, as a representative of the world, the Athenian world, that is, a man, Euthyphro. His character is best unfolded by the dialogue itself. He is what we might term a religionist—a man of forms and ceremonies, of an antiquated and outrageous theology, and of incurable prejudice. Plato introduces him to us as a prosecutor in a suit of painful grotesqueness—the prosecution of his own father for murder.

To explain this apparently outrageous conception, we must suggest that Plato has taken Euthyphro as a type of the Athenians themselves, and is attempting to put before the Athenians their own inconsistency, and has donned for the nonce the comic mask of Aristophanes. Just as, in the comedy of *The Clouds*, Aristophanes had represented a son beating his father as a result of sophistic teaching, so here Plato would remind the Athenians that their own theology and legislation can be, and is, brought to an absurdity and a caricature in the hands of its bigoted and unthinking professors. Socrates in this dialogue says, in effect : " You persecute me for impiety, so be it; but are you free from the charge of impiety yourselves, Athenians? The tales, the immoral and blasphemous tales, which make up a large part of your religion, so called, are impiety, not my teaching, which would drive such abominations out of religion, and which you call radical, unconstitutional, and corrupting."

In Euthyphro then we have a picture of the conservative Athenian who is perfectly satisfied with his own religion, no matter into what glaring absurdities it may lead him. Now to see in what manner Socrates encounters this incarnation of bigotry and into what questions he attempts to lead the mind of the bigot. The main idea running through the *Euthyphro* would seem to be of this tenor. To define piety is impossible; we cannot *say* what is holy, but we can act it; and therefore let every man try to be pious and serve God, and not lay down the law about piety. Euthyphro, on the contrary, is quite ready to define piety or anything else with which religion is concerned, and Socrates, in his usual way, humours him and requests a definition. But the definition given is soon shown to be inadequate, and another is requested, and a third. In the first, Euthyphro says, " Piety is doing what I am now doing." Next, " Piety is that which is dear to the gods, or to all the gods." Thirdly, " Piety is attention to the gods." And when for the third time he is shown to have given an inadequate rule of piety, he does not take his failure to heart; he does not say, " I confess I know nothing certain about piety; pray teach me." No! he is content to leave certain knowledge alone, and go on in his own pretentious and superficial creed. He goes his way into the law court to contest against his own father the law as he reads it, and Socrates goes his; not however to contest in a law court, but to search the wide world for an answer to his unceasing inquiry, " What is Right? Is there a man on earth who can tell me?" until the Athenians weary of this questioner who is a reproach to their city and their creed, silencing his eloquent and earnest converse in the tomb.

ANALYSIS.

Eu. What has brought you to the law court, Socrates?

Soc. An impeachment of corrupting the youth, Euthyphro, preferred by one Meletus, a clever lad; he is reforming the state, and begins by reforming me. He says I make new gods.

Eu. Ah! the Athenians will not listen to what I have to say on that subject; they laugh.

Soc. I wish they would only laugh, if they would hear as well. Well, and what is your suit?

Eu. I am prosecuting my father for murder.

Soc. Good heavens! What a theologian, if you can do that without fear of heaven's vengeance!

Eu. My dear Socrates, in a case of right and wrong, relationship has no place. My father killed a hired servant (a murderer himself) by wilfully neglecting him in chains.

Soc. Then if you are so certain that you are right, be my champion and be my reference; when they prosecute me, I will say, Here is Euthyphro, he knows that I am not wrong; fight out the question with him. Now tell me what is holiness and unholiness.

Eu. That which I am now doing in my prosecution, Socrates, is holy, just as Zeus acted towards Cronus, and Cronus towards Ouranus.

Soc. Why! do you believe all that? Do you think the gods fought and quarrelled as people say?

Eu. Certainly I do.

Soc. Really. But you didn't tell me what holiness is—you said, "This particular thing is holy." Now that doesn't tell me what holiness is. What is the general definition of holiness?

Eu. Oh! holiness is that which is dear to the gods, and *vice versâ.*

Soc. Stay! You said that the gods disputed, did you not? Then how are we to know, if they dispute, what is holy and what is unholy, for they will have different opinions? And it is not on minor questions, just as if you and I were to differ on a question of dates, but on the most important questions of faith and morals that they will differ.

Eu. They could never differ about justice being done, for instance.

Soc. No more do men; they are all anxious for justice to be done. The difficulty is what is the right? what is justice? When they are agreed on that, men and gods, they will do it, and not before. So you have not given me a rule for finding holiness. Shall we say what *all* the gods love is holy, and what they all detest, unholy!

Eu. Yes.

Soc. Is the holy loved by the gods because holy, or holy because loved by the gods?

Eu. I don't follow.

Soc. Try in this way: everything borne, led, seen, become, loved, implies something that bears, leads, sees, makes, loves. And this something is prior to the other. Therefore, "the gods love," is a prior notion to "loved by the gods." Therefore also the gods do not love because a thing is god-beloved; they love a thing for some other reason.   And this other reason will imply a notion prior to the gods loving, just as the gods loving is prior to the notion god-beloved.

Then if you grant that the gods love holiness because it is holy, we shall have these three notions in order of priority and extension :—

(1) Holiness.
(2) The gods loving.
(3) God-beloved.

From these we will draw our deductions.   And I am proving that holiness is not merely the same as god-beloved, as you say.   For,

(1) If holiness and god-beloved were the same,
Then holiness would be a posterior notion to the gods loving ;
But holiness is a prior notion to the gods loving.
Therefore it is not the same with the god-beloved.

(2) If the god-beloved and holiness were the same,
Then the god-beloved would be a prior notion to gods loving ;
But the god-beloved has been proved to be a posterior notion to gods loving,
Therefore it is not the same with holiness.

So that you have not defined me holiness even now.

Eu. You are a Dædalus ; you make the argument act like a moving creature.

Soc. No, it is you ; but let us go on.   Justice and holiness are not the same thing, are they ?   All holiness is just ; but it does not follow that all justice is holy. Just as it is true that all reverence implies fear ; but not true that all fear implies reverence.

Cannot we then get a definition of holiness, by seeing what part of justice it is.

Eu. Oh, yes; holiness is that justice which attends to the gods.

Soc. Attends to them? As men attend to dogs and horses, &c., to make them better and finer. But how do we make the gods better and finer; or help them to do great deeds, as the physicians' art helps them to cure sick people?

Eu. I don't know. If you do your duty in the way of sacrifices and prayers, you will be prosperous and you will be holy.

Soc. Oh! I see; holiness is the science of giving and taking with the gods, a sort of business?

Eu. Business, if you like—we give them honour and glory.

Soc. Things that please them, in fact.

Eu. Certainly.

Soc. Ah! but we proved that holiness was not that which pleased the gods, the god-beloved, in fact.

Eu. Daedalus again; you have brought it round once more. I must be off. Good morning.

Soc. Alack! alack! I thought I was to be told how to live and please heaven.

ΠΛΑΤΩΝΟΣ ΕΥΘΥΦΡΩΝ.

CAP. I.

Steph.

Τί ιεώτερον, ὦ Σώκρατες, γέγονεν, ὅτι σὺ τὰς ἐν
Λυκείῳ καταλιπὼν διατριβὰς ἐνθάδε νῦν διατρίβεις 2
περὶ τὴν τοῦ βασιλέως στοάν; οὐ γάρ που καὶ σοί
γε δίκη τις οὖσα τυγχάνει πρὸς τὸν βασιλέα ὥσπερ
ἐμοί.

ΣΩ. Οὗτοι δὴ Ἀθηναῖοί γε, ὦ Εὐθύφρον, δίκην
αὐτὴν καλοῦσιν, ἀλλὰ γραφήν.

νεώτερον. Stallbaum finds this use of the comparative, i.e., newer than we already have, " novo novius," especially natural to the Athenians, who were always telling or hearing some new thing. But forms like "sæpius" will illustrate it better.

ἐν Λυκείῳ . . . sc. γυμνασίῳ. The colonnades of the gymnasia were the resort of philosophers. This gymnasium was so called from the neighbouring temple of Apollo Lyceus.

διατριβάς. This word seems to combine the meanings of haunts and pursuits. The latter is preferable.

βασιλέως στοάν. The στοά is that of Zeus Eleutherius; the βασιλεύς is that archon whose duties were religious, who pre-

sided over prosecutions for impiety or murder. Compare Theaetetus ad fin., νῦν μὲν οὖν ἀπαντητέον μοι εἰς τὴν τοῦ βασιλέως στοάν ἐπὶ τὴν Μελήτου γραφὴν ἥν με γέγραπται. (The Lyceum and Eleutherium were at opposite points of the city.)

καὶ σοί γε . . . οὖσα τυγχάνει. "You have not, I suppose, as well as I . . ."

οὐ . . . δίκην . . . ἀλλὰ γραφήν. γραφή is used only of a public prosecution, under which head fell those tried by the βασιλεύς: δίκη is the general term. Its first sense (which we find in the next sentence) is "bill of accusation," lodged with the magistrate. Thus γέγραπται, "has had a bill entered," middle voice.

c 2

ΕΥΘ. Τί φής; γραφὴν σέ τις, ὡς ἔοικε, γέγραπται; οὐ γὰρ ἐκεῖνό γε καταγνώσομαι, ὡς σύ γε
ἕτερον;

B ΣΩ. Οὐ γὰρ οὖν.

ΕΥΘ. Ἀλλὰ σὲ ἄλλος;

ΣΩ. Πάνυ γε.

ΕΥΘ. Τίς οὗτος;

ΣΩ. Οὐδ' αὐτὸς πάνυ τι γιγνώσκω, ὦ Εὐθύφρον,
τὸν ἄνδρα· νέος γάρ τίς μοι φαίνεται καὶ ἀγνώς·
ὀνομάζουσι μέντοι αὐτόν, ὡς ἐγῷμαι, Μέλητον. ἔστι
δὲ τὸν δῆμον Πιτθεύς, εἴ τινα νῷ ἔχεις Πιτθέα Μέλητον, οἷον τετανότριχα καὶ οὐ πάνυ εὐγένειον, ἐπίγρυπον δέ.

ΕΥΘ. Οὐκ ἐννοῶ, ὦ Σώκρατες. ἀλλὰ δὴ τίνα
γραφήν σε γέγραπται;

C ΣΩ. Ἥντινα; οὐκ ἀγεννῆ, ὥς ἔμοιγε δοκεῖ· τὸ γὰρ

B. οὐ γάρ, &c. "For I will
not suspect you of bringing an
action against any one." Lit.,
"For I will not think that badly
of you (as might be vulgarly
said) that you are accusing
another."

οὖν. If there is any logical
sequence in the use of this particle, we must understand some
such ellipse as, "You know me
well, and so cannot suspect me
of that," i.e. "of course not."
Notice that πάνυ τι is generally found with a negative.

ἀγνώς, passive, "obscure."

μέντοι, adversative particle.
"But his name ..."

ἔστι δὲ τὸν δῆμον, called by
Jelf (579, 4) the adverbial accusative, because it limits or de-
fines the verbal notion of being.
Cf. Her. 6, 83, Κλέανδρος γένος
ἐὼν Φιγαλεὺς ἀπ' Ἀρκαδίης.

εἴ τινα νῷ ἔχεις. "If you re-
member." Thus Socrates in the
Republic (490 A), when re-
capitulating, says ἡγεῖτο δέ, εἰ
νῷ ἔχεις, ἀλήθεια.

οἷον τετ., i.e. τοιοῦτον ὅς ἐστι
τετανόθριξ, cf. Thuc. 7, 21, πρὸς
ἄνδρας τολμηροὺς, οἵους καὶ
Ἀθηναίους, and Soph. Trach. 443,
πῶς δ' οὐ χἀτέρας (sc. ἄρχει)
οἵας γ' ἐμοῦ. It is a species of the
common attraction of the relative
to the case of the antecedent.

τετανότ. with long straight
hair. οὐ πάνυ εὐγ. implying
youth.

ἐπίγρυπον. Cf. 474 Rep. C.,
τοῦ δὲ τὸ γρύπον βασιλικόν φατε
εἶναι.

ἥντινα, &c. Through this
statement of Socrates runs a
vein of that quiet but suggestive
and biting irony in which he
is unequalled. This is not

νέον ὄντα τοσοῦτον πρᾶγμα ἐγνωκέναι οὐ φαῦλόν
ἐστιν. ἐκεῖνος γάρ, ὥς φησιν, οἶδε, τίνα τρόπον οἱ
νέοι διαφθείρονται καὶ τίνες οἱ διαφθείροντες αὐτούς.
καὶ κινδυνεύει σοφός τις εἶναι· καὶ τὴν ἐμὴν ἀμαθίαν
κατιδὼν ὡς διαφθείροντος τοὺς ἡλικιώτας αὐτοῦ,
ἔρχεται κατηγορήσων μου, ὥσπερ πρὸς μητέρα, πρὸς
τὴν πόλιν. καὶ φαίνεταί μοι τῶν πολιτικῶν μόνος
ἄρχεσθαι ὀρθῶς· ὀρθῶς γάρ ἐστι τῶν νέων πρῶτον D)
ἐπιμεληθῆναι, ὅπως ἔσονται ὅ τι ἄριστοι, ὥσπερ
γεωργὸν ἀγαθὸν τῶν νέων φυτῶν εἰκὸς πρῶτον ἐπιμεληθῆναι, μετὰ δὲ τοῦτο καὶ τῶν ἄλλων· καὶ δὴ
καὶ Μέλητος ἴσως πρῶτον μὲν ἡμᾶς ἐκκαθαίρει, τοὺς
τῶν νέων τὰς βλάστας διαφθείροντας, ὥς φησιν·
ἔπειτα μετὰ τοῦτο δῆλον, ὅτι τῶν πρεσβυτέρων

εἰρωνεία, which was a dialectical process.
C. τὸ ... ἐγνωκέναι. These words form the subject of the sentence : "A young man determining upon such an important step." But translate, "It is no mean enterprise for a young man," &c.
διαφθ. This corrupting influence must usually be taken of the moral side of a man's nature, though it trenches sometimes on the intellectual.
ὡς διαφθ. Understand ἐμοῦ from ἐμήν.
πρὸς τὴν μητέρα. So Thrasymachus, in the Republic, when he is angered with Socrates for worsting him in argument, says, "Have you a nurse, Socrates ?" Εἰπέ μοι, ἔφη, ὦ Σώκρατες, τίτθη σοί ἐστιν ;
πολιτικῶν. Jowett, "our political men." Stallb. and Matthiae, "politics." The latter seems preferable, which will then depend on ἄρχεσθαι.

D. ὀρθῶς γάρ ... Supply πολιτικῶν ἄρχεσθαι, "For the right way to begin .... is to.. "
ἐπιμεληθῆναι. The middle here should be brought out ; its force, "apply one's self to," c.g.
ἔσονται. Notice this realistic future (instead of an ordinary conjunctive) pointing to the certain result of a proper training.
εἰκός, sc. ἔστι.
καὶ δὴ καὶ Μέλητος. "Well then, Meletus also," sc. in his moral and political husbandry : the particles mark the transition from the simile to the reality.
ἴσως. Here again the sarcasm peeps out = "no doubt."
τὰς βλάστας. Keeping up the metaphor, "these young sprigs."
ἐκκαθ. This word, from the special sense of cleansing, has come to be applied to any removal of superfluous or objectionable matter, and is used of finishing a statue, ridding a land

ἐπιμεληθεὶς πλείστων καὶ μεγίστων ἀγαθῶν αἴτιος
τῇ πόλει γενήσεται, ὥς γε τὸ εἰκὸς ξυμβῆναι ἐκ
τοιαύτης ἀρχῆς ἀρξαμένῳ.

CAP. II.

ΕΥΘ. Βουλοίμην ἄν, ὦ Σώκρατες, ἀλλ' ὀρρωδῶ,
μὴ τοὐναντίον γένηται. ἀτεχνῶς γάρ μοι δοκεῖ ἀφ'
ἑστίας ἄρχεσθαι κακουργεῖν τὴν πόλιν, ἐπιχειρῶν
ἀδικεῖν σέ. καί μοι λέγε, τί καὶ ποιοῦντά σέ φησι
διαφθείρειν τοὺς νέους;

B ΣΩ. Ἄτοπα, ὦ˜θαυμάσιε, ὡς οὕτω γ' ἀκοῦσαι.
φησὶ γάρ με ποιητὴν εἶναι θεῶν, καὶ ὡς καινούς
ποιοῦντα θεούς, τοὺς δ' ἀρχαίους οὐ νομίζοντα ἐγράψατο τούτων αὐτῶν ἕνεκα, ὥς φησιν.

ΕΥΘ. Μανθάνω, ὦ Σώκρατες· ὅτι δὴ σὺ τὸ

δαιμόνιον φῂς σαυτῷ ἑκάστοτε γίγνεσθαι. ὡς οὖν
καινοτομοῦντός σου περὶ τὰ θεῖα γέγραπται ταύτην
τὴν γραφήν, καὶ ὡς διαβαλῶν δὴ ἔρχεται εἰς τὸ δι-
καστήριον, εἰδὼς ὅτι εὐδιάβολα τὰ τοιαῦτα πρὸς
τοὺς πολλούς. καὶ ἐμοῦ γάρ τοι, ὅταν τι λέγω ἐν τῇ C
ἐκκλησίᾳ περὶ τῶν θείων, προλέγων αὐτοῖς τὰ μέλ-
λοντα, καταγελῶσιν ὡς μαινομένου· καίτοι οὐδὲν ὅ
τι οὐκ ἀληθὲς εἴρηκα ὧν προεῖπον· ἀλλ' ὅμως φθο-
νοῦσιν ἡμῖν πᾶσι τοῖς τοιούτοις. ἀλλ' οὐδὲν αὐτῶν
χρὴ φροντίζειν, ἀλλ' ὁμόσε ἰέναι.

ἑκάστοτε, "on each occasion."
Thus we find it put in the same
sentence with ἀεί, Ar. Nub.,
1279—

πότερα νομίζεις καινὸν ἀεὶ τὸν
Δία
ὕειν ὕδωρ ἑκάστοτ', ἤ . . . (i.e.
"every time he does rain.")

This rendering agrees with the
intermittent and unoriginative
character of the δαιμόνιον.
καινοτομοῦντος. The idea involved in this word is that of
cutting *into* something afresh.
Observe the vowel variation of
this and other roots in different
combinations. Thus—
Verb pres.—ει, ε, or α: τέμνω,
βάλλω, σπείρω.
Verb aor.—α: ἔταμον, ἔβαλον,
ἔσπαρον.
Verb comp. — o: καινοτομέω,
διάβολος, ὁμόσπορος.
In translating, make two sentences of the passage: thus

Jowett, "He thinks you are a
neologian ; and he is going to
have you up before the court for
this."
ὡς διαβαλ . . . ἔρχεται, "He
seems to be *going* to play the
part of a traducer."
C. ὧν προεῖπον. A common
attraction of the relative to the
case of the antecedent. Cf.
Thuc. 7, 21, ἄγων ἀπὸ τῶν πό-
λεων ὧν ἔπεισε στρατιάν.
ἀλλά . . . ἀλλά. The first is
adversative of the clause καίτοι
. . ., the second of both clauses
preceding taken together, and
might be translated, " Well !
we mustn't pay heed . . ."
ὁμόσε ἰέναι. Latin : cominus
pugnare, "come to close quar-
ters." Cf. Thuc. 2, 62, ὁμόσε
ἰέναι τοῖς ἐχθροῖς, and Ar. Eccl.
863, βαδιστέον ὁμόσ' ἐοσί, and
Dem. Dionysod. 12 δδ, 14, ὡς
ἑώρα ἡμᾶς ὁμόσε πορευομένους,
" When he saw us going straight
at him, ready to prosecute," i.e.

CAP. III.

ΣΩ. Ὦ φίλε Εὐθύφρον, ἀλλὰ τὸ μὲν καταγελασ-
θῆναι ἴσως οὐδὲν πρᾶγμα. Ἀθηναίοις γάρ τοι, ὡς
ἐμοὶ δοκεῖ, οὐ σφόδρα μέλει, ἄν τινα δεινὸν οἴωνται

D εἶναι, μὴ μέντοι διδασκαλικὸν τῆς αὐτοῦ σοφίας· ὃν
δ᾽ ἂν καὶ ἄλλους οἴωνται ποιεῖν τοιούτους, θυμοῦνται,
εἴτ᾽ οὖν φθόνῳ, ὡς σὺ λέγεις, εἴτε δι᾽ ἄλλο τι.

ΕΥΘ. Τούτου οὖν πέρι ὅπως ποτὲ πρὸς ἐμὲ
ἔχουσιν, οὐ πάνυ ἐπιθυμῶ πειραθῆναι. ·

ΣΩ. Ἴσως γὰρ σὺ μὲν δοκεῖς σπάνιον σεαυτὸν
παρέχειν καὶ διδάσκειν οὐκ ἐθέλειν τὴν σεαυτοῦ σο-
φίαν· ἐγὼ δὲ φοβοῦμαι, μὴ ὑπὸ φιλανθρωπίας δοκῶ

ἴσως οὐδέν πρ. So Gorg. 447,
B, οὐδὲν πρᾶγμα, ὦ Σώκρατες, ἐγὼ
γὰρ καὶ ἰάσομαι.

δεινόν. This word expresses a
quality on which the Athenians
prided themselves, viz. that of
skill and daring combined. Cf.
the description of the chariot-
race in Electra, Soph., 731, γνοὺς
δ᾽ οὐξ Ἀθηνῶν δεινὸς ἡνιοστρόφος,
"And the daring charioteer
from Athens seeing it . . ."
Compare the whole description of
Athenian aggression and daring
in Thucydides, 1, 68, seqq.

D. μὴ μέντοι διδασκ. "Pro-
vided that he be not anxious to
impart his knowledge, learn-
ing." μή introduces a supposi-
tion, not a fact.

ποιεῖν, sc. τοιοῦτον. "But if
they think any man of this kind
is making others like himself."

εἴτ᾽ οὖν φθόνῳ. Cf. Pericles'
criticism of Athenian audiences,
Thuc. 2, 35, ὅτε γὰρ ξυνειδὼς καὶ
εὔνους ἀκροατὴς τάχ᾽ ἄν τι ἐνδε-
εστέρως πρὸς ἃ βούλεταί τε καὶ
ἐπίσταται νομίσειε δηλοῦσθαι, ὅτε

ἄπειρός ἐστιν ἅ καὶ πλεονάζεσθαι,
διὰ φθόνον εἴ τι ὑπὲρ τὴν ἑαυτοῦ
φύσιν ἀκούοι.

ὃν δ᾽ ἄν . . . θυμοῦνται. Omission
of the demonstrative object after
θυμοῦνται. We should expect ἐὰν
δέ τινα οἴωνται .. τούτῳ θυμοῦνται.
The construction is due to the
synthetic tendency which avoids
a demonstrative where the sense
can be preserved in a continuous
relative clause.

ὡς σὺ λέγεις. Here we notice
Socrates guarding against a conclusion that is open to question.
He never takes anything for
granted that admits of question
or of further substantiation.

σπάνιον σεαυτ. ποιεῖν. Jowett
paraphrases, "You are select
in your acquaintance." Lit.,
"make yourself rare," or "difficult of access."

ὑπὸ φιλ. Explanatory, gives
the reason. Lat., quae mea est
comitas : it does not strike the
Athenians so ; it is put in paren-
thetically so by Socrates to show
why he teaches. ·

αὐτοῖς ὅ τί περ ἔχω ἐκκεχυμένως παντὶ ἀνδρὶ λέγειν,
οὐ μόνον ἄνευ μισθοῦ, ἀλλὰ καὶ προστιθεὶς ἂν ἡδέως,
εἴ τις μου ἐθέλοι ἀκούειν. εἰ μὲν οὖν, ὃ νῦν δὴ ἔλεγον,
μέλλοιέν μου καταγελᾶν, ὥσπερ σὺ φῂς σαυτοῦ, Ε
οὐδὲν ἂν εἴη ἀηδὲς παίζοντας καὶ γελῶντας ἐν τῷ
δικαστηρίῳ διαγαγεῖν, εἰ δὲ σπουδάσονται, τοῦτ᾽ ἤδη
ὅπῃ ἀποβήσεται ἄδηλον πλὴν ὑμῖν τοῖς μάντεσιν.

ΕΥΘ. Ἀλλ᾽ ἴσως οὐδὲν ἔσται, ὦ Σώκρατες, πρᾶγμα, ἀλλὰ σύ τε κατὰ νοῦν ἀγωνιεῖ τὴν δίκην, οἶμαι
δὲ καὶ ἐμὲ τὴν ἐμήν.

CAP IV.

ΣΩ. Ἔστι δὲ δὴ σοι, ὦ Εὐθύφρον, τις ἡ δικη ;
φεύγεις αὐτὴν ἢ διώκεις ;

δοκῶ αὐτοῖς, "I am known,"
"I have the reputation."
ἄνευ μισθοῦ. This was one of
the great differences between
Socrates and the ordinary so-
phist. Cf. Rep. 337, D., where
Thrasymachus says they cannot
expect him to expound his views
for nothing. ἀλλὰ πρὸς τῷ μαθεῖν
καὶ ἀπότισον ἀργύριον.
ἀλλὰ καί. Here we pass into
the sphere of the potential : the
potential particle ἂν is employed,
and the verb historic conjunctive. Expanded, "εἰ τις ἐθέλοι
ἀκούειν, μίσθον προστιθείη ἄν."
Other neuter verbs of the kind
are, κερδαίνειν, to gain ; ξυμβάλ-
λεσθαι, to contribute, &c., Stallb.
οὐδὲν ἂν εἴη. Notice Socrates'
lofty indifference to human
weakness, if he can only obtain
any sort of hearing for his
gospel.
E. ὅπῃ ἀπόβησεται. Quo sci-
licet modo eventurum sit.

ἔδηλον, &c. Socrates seems
here to betray an expectation
that the movement bodes no
good to him ; veiling it in the
usual Greek fashion with a
euphemistic obscurity of expression.
φ. αὐτήν. "Are you being prosecuted in your suit ?" Acc. of
respect or further limitation.
Cf. Ar. Eq., 617, πῶς τὸ πρᾶγμ'
ἀγωνίσω; and Dem. 653, 25,
γραφὴν ἀγωνίζεσθαι. To be en-
gaged in a matter, a trial. So
here, "Are you defendant or
prosecutor in your suit ?" Or,
to explain it thus :—In such an
expression the acc. will be found
to be the case in which the substantive ordinarily occurs in
kindred expressions : e.g., δίκην
or γραφὴν, γράφεσθαι, &c. And
it may then be transferred by
analogy to intransitive verbs
such as διώκω, φεύγω.

ΕΥΘ. Διώκω.

ΣΩ. Τίνα;

4 ΕΥΘ. Ὃν διώκων αὖ δοκῶ μαίνεσθαι.

ΣΩ. Τί δαί; πετόμενόν τινα διώκεις;

ΕΥΘ. Πολλοῦ γε δεῖ πέτεσθαι, ὅς γε τυγχάνει ὢν εὖ μάλα πρεσβύτης.

ΣΩ. Τίς οὗτος;

ΕΥΘ. Ὁ ἐμὸς πατήρ.

ΣΩ. Ὁ σός, ὦ βέλτιστε;

ΕΥΘ. Πάνυ μὲν οὖν.

ΣΩ. Ἔστι δὲ τί τὸ ἔγκλημα καὶ τίνος ἡ δίκη;

ΕΥΘ. Φόνου, ὦ Σώκρατες;

ΣΩ. Ἡράκλεις· ἦ που, ὦ Εὐθύφρον, ἀγνοεῖται ὑπὸ τῶν πολλῶν ὅπῃ ποτὲ ὀρθῶς ἔχει. οὐ γὰρ
Β οἶμαί γε τοῦ ἐπιτυχόντος εἶναι ὀρθῶς αὐτὸ πρᾶξαι, ἀλλὰ πόρρω που ἤδη σοφίας ἐλαύνοντος.

ΕΥΘ. Πόρρω μέντοι νὴ Δί᾽, ὦ Σώκρατες.

ὃν διώκων. Notice again this synthetic construction.

πετόμενον. A double sense is here intended. For the word means besides "flying" (the ordinary sense), to move swiftly. Cf. εἰώθαμεν λέγειν ἐπὶ τῶν ταχέως τρεχόντων, ὅτι πέτονται; and Rep. 567, D., πολλοὶ ἥξουσι πετόμενοι, said of people gathering quickly towards an object.

πολλοῦ, gen. privative, acc. to Jelf. Matthiae explains it as a genitive of distance from, applicable strictly to the first meaning of the verb, but transferred to its secondary sense. Jowett, "Nay, he is not very volatile at his time of life."

ἦ που. "Asseverationem ἦ cum dubitatione που significant," Stallb. "Certainly," or "surely, I should think."

ὅπῃ ποτὲ ὀρθῶς ἔχει, "what is right." Lit., where the case stands right on any occasion (ποτέ). So οὕτως ἔχει, κακῶς ἔχει, &c., &c.

τοῦ ἐπιτυχόντος. Cf. Rep. 352, C., οὐ γὰρ περὶ τοῦ ἐπιτυχόντος ὁ λόγος, ἀλλὰ περὶ τοῦ ὅντινα τρόπον χρὴ ζῆν. "The question does not treat of a chance subject." So here, "a chance person," "any one."

Β. σοφίας. For this genitive, cf. Lysides, 204, D., πόρρω ἤδη εἶ πορευόμενος τοῦ ἔρωτος; and Ar. Ran. 35—
καὶ γὰρ ἐγγὺς τῆς θύρας Ἤδη
βαδίζων εἰμί.

μέντοι. If we are to find any adversative force in this particle here, we must suppose such an ellipsis as, "But (of course I see) they must certainly be."

ΣΩ. Ἔστι δὲ δὴ τῶν οἰκείων τις ὁ τεθνεὼς ὑπὸ
τοῦ σοῦ πατρός; ἢ δῆλα δή· οὐ γὰρ ἄν που ὑπέρ γε
ἀλλοτρίου ἐπεξήεισθα φόνου αὐτῷ.

ΕΥΘ. Γελοῖον, ὦ Σώκρατες, ὅτι οἴει τι διαφέρειν
εἴτε ἀλλότριος εἴτε οἰκεῖος ὁ τεθνεώς, ἀλλ᾽ οὐ τοῦτο
μόνον δεῖν φυλάττειν, εἴτε ἐν δίκῃ ἔκτεινεν ὁ κτείνας
εἴτε μή, καὶ εἰ μὲν ἐν δίκῃ, ἐᾶν, εἰ δὲ μή, ἐπεξιέναι, Ϲ
ἐάν περ ὁ κτείνας συνέστιός σοι καὶ ὁμοτράπεζος ᾖ.
ἴσον γὰρ τὸ μίασμα γίγνεται, ἐὰν ξυνῇς τῷ τοιούτῳ
ξυνειδώς, καὶ μὴ ἀφοσιοῖς σεαυτόν τε καὶ ἐκεῖνον τῇ
δίκῃ ἐπεξιών. ἐπεὶ ὅγε ἀποθανὼν πελάτης τις ἦν .

τῶν οἰκειων τις. For Socrates would not suppose Euthyphro capable of pushing such an accusation against his father unless the plea of family satisfaction at least could be urged. τεθνέως. This participle is formed analogically from a syncopated form of the perfect. So we find ἕσταμεν, τέθνατον, τέθναμεν, ἑστώς, πεπτῶτος, &c. Γελοῖον, &c. This sentence requires careful analysis. The words ἀλλ᾽ οὐ τοῦτο, seqq., give *Euthyphro's view of what ought to be done* in the case of a murder, he having dismissed Socrates' suggestion in the words γελοῖον ... τεθνεώς. But we must notice that οὐ refers to Socrates' mistaken view of the case, and does not belong to δεῖν φυλάττειν. Leaving it out, we might paraphrase, "Whilst the true course is to notice," &c. For the legal question, v. fin. Note. ἐάν περ ... ξυνέστιος ... The revolting idea of a son proceeding against a father for such a crime will appear less repulsive, though hardly less dreadful, if we call to mind the intense belief of the

Greeks in an actual Nemesis or "providence of retribution." The extreme and typical instance of this is the murder of Clytemnaestra by her son Orestes, which, it will be remembered, was solemnly justified by the testimony of a goddess. Aesch. Eum. Stallbaum adds another motive for the proceeding, viz., the fear of being implicated in the crime; a view which he fortifies with an apt quotation from Hor. 3, i. 11, Od. :—

" Vetabo qui Cereris sacrum
Volgarit arcana, sub isdem
Sit trabibus fragilemve
mecum
Solvat phaselon. Sæpe Diespiter
Neglectus *incesto addidit inte-
grum.*"

ἴσον. Sc. to you as to him. Ϲ. ἀφοσιοῖς. Conjunctive *prim.* notice. πελάτης. These were attached to the soil, not actual slaves, but received a sixth of the produce they raised for their hirers. Hence called ἐκτήμοροι, ἐργολάβοι, θῆτες, villeins or serfs.

ἐμός, καὶ ὡς ἐγεωργοῦμεν ἐν τῇ Νάξῳ, ἐθήτευεν ἐκεῖ
παρ᾽ ἡμῖν. παροινήσας οὖν καὶ ὀργισθεὶς τῶν οἰκετῶν τινὶ τῶν ἡμετέρων ἀποσφάττει αὐτόν. ὁ οὖν
πατὴρ ξυνδήσας τοὺς πόδας καὶ τὰς χεῖρας αὐτοῦ,
D καταβαλὼν εἰς τάφρον τινά, πέμπει δεῦρο ἄνδρα
πευσόμενον τοῦ ἐξηγητοῦ ὅ τι χρὴ ποιεῖν. ἐν δὲ
τούτῳ τῷ χρόνῳ τοῦ δεδεμένου ὠλιγώρει τε καὶ
ἠμέλει ὡς ἀνδροφόνου καὶ οὐδὲν ὂν πρᾶγμα, εἰ καὶ
ἀποθάνοι· ὅπερ οὖν καὶ ἔπαθεν. ὑπὸ γὰρ λιμοῦ καὶ
ῥίγους καὶ τῶν δεσμῶν ἀποθνήσκει πρὶν τὸν ἄγγελον
παρὰ τοῦ ἐξηγητοῦ ἀφικέσθαι. ταῦτα δὴ οὖν καὶ
ἀγανακτεῖ ὅ τε πατὴρ καὶ οἱ ἄλλοι οἰκεῖοι, ὅτι ἐγὼ
ὑπὲρ τοῦ ἀνδροφόνου τῷ πατρὶ φόνου ἐπεξέρχομαι,
οὔτε ἀποκτείναντι, ὥς φασιν ἐκεῖνοι, οὔτ᾽ εἰ ὅ τι

ἐν Νάξῳ. Such an occupation
(of a conquered territory) was
called a κληρουχία, and the holder
κληροῦχος, or γεώμορος. For
the account of this colonisation,
v. Thuc. 1, 98, compared with
Plut. Pericl. ii.
οἰκετῶν. These were the regular bought slaves, domestics.
D. ἐξηγητοῦ. Used of an
expounder of oracles in Herodotus. At Athens their duties
were monopolised by the Eumolpidae, the guardians of traditional, unwritten law or
usage ; their nearest counterpart
were the jurists of Rome, cf.
Dem. Euerg. 1160, ἦλθον ὡς
τοὺς ἐξηγητὰς ἵνα εἰδείην ὅτι
με χρὴ ποιεῖν περὶ τούτων.
ὠλιγώρει. The latter part of
this word is said to be akin to
Lat. cura. Gk. οὖρος, a guard,
cf. Ἄρκτουρος, vereor, ward,
ware, guard. We can certainly
trace other words through exactly the same changes, e.g. :—

Gk.	Lat.	Eng.
οἶνος	vinum	wine
ἰτέα	vitis	withy
	vimen	
	vieo	
αἶ	vae	woe
ἔργον		work

οὐδὲν ὂν π. V.S. 3 fin. for the
expression : a curious though
common absolute accusatival
construction, paralleled by Rep.
426 C. προαγορεύουσι τοῖς πολί-
ταις τὴν κατάστασιν τῆς πόλεως
ὅλην μὴ κινεῖν, ὡς ἀποθανούμενον,
ὅς ἂν τοῦτο δρᾷ. See also 604
B, κάλλιστον ἡσυχίαν ἄγειν ἐν
ξυμφοραῖς, ὡς οὐδὲν προβαῖνον
τῷ χαλεπῶς φέροντι.
τῶν δεσμῶν, "the manacles
he had on him," his chains.
So in French, la tête, his head.
οὔτ᾽ ἀποκτείναντι... οὔτ᾽, &c.
The speaker is here hurried into
some confusion of language by
his vehement statement. Lit.
"who has neither killed him,

μάλιστ' ἀπέκτεινεν, ἀνδροφόνου γε ὄντος τοῦ ἀποθανόντος, οὐ δεῖν φροντίζειν ὑπὲρ τοῦ τοιούτου· ἀνό- Ε
σιον γὰρ εἶναι τὸ υἱὸν πατρὶ φόνου ἐπεξιέναι· κακῶς
εἰδότες, ὦ Σώκρατες, τὸ θεῖον ὡς ἔχει τοῦ ὁσίου τε
πέρι καὶ τοῦ ἀνοσίου.

ΣΩ. Σὺ δὲ δὴ πρὸς Διός, ὦ Εὐθύφρον, οὑτωσὶ
ἀκριβῶς οἴει ἐπίστασθαι περὶ τῶν θείων, ὅπη ἔχει,
καὶ τῶν ὁσίων τε καὶ ἀνοσίων, ὥστε τούτων οὕτω
πραχθέντων, ὡς σὺ λέγεις, οὐ φοβεῖ δικαζόμενος τῷ
πατρί, ὅπως μὴ αὖ σὺ ἀνόσιον πρᾶγμα τυγχάνῃς
πράττων;

ΕΥΘ. Οὐδὲν γὰρ ἄν μου ὄφελος εἴη, ὦ Σώκρατες, 5
οὐδέ τῳ ἂν διαφέροι Εὐθύφρων τῶν πολλῶν ἀνθρώπων, εἰ μὴ τὰ τοιαῦτα πάντα ἀκριβῶς εἰδείην.

so they say, nor, even if he had, should one give thought to a murderous wretch like the deceased." The second οὔτε begins an entirely fresh sentence, although corresponding logically to the first οὔτε, which stands before a subordinate clause; and so we should expect another dependent sentence after the second οὔτε to this effect : "Nor, even if he had, properly liable to punishment for murdering such a wretch as this." οὐ before δεῖν is merely intensitive according to the common practice of using more negatives to emphasize denial.

E. πρὸς Διός, "before," i.e. "by Zeus."

ὥστε, &c. Notice the sequence;—οἴει ἐπίστασθαι... ὥστε οὐ φοβεῖ ... ὅπως μὴ ... τυγχάνῃς.

αὖ, "in your turn," i.e. be committing impiety yourself whilst accusing your father of impiety.

Οὐδὲν γάρ. Elliptical. "No! For then . . ." The phrase means, "I should be good for nothing," cf. Laws, 856 C, πᾶς δὲ ἀνήρ, οὗ καὶ σμικρὸν ὄφελος, ἐνδεικνύτω ταῖς ἀρχαῖς. The pretence of astonishment on the part of Socrates in the former sentence is meant to draw out from Euthyphro this unqualified assumption of theological omniscience. It is then assumed as a basis for a string of deductions, inevitably ending in the conclusion, "which is absurd," just as Euclid starts with his impossible assumption in a reductio ad absurdum. For the use of the proper name instead of ἐγώ, cf. Virg. Aen. i. 48, "et quisquam numen Junonis adoret praeterea?" where Juno herself is the speaker.

CAP. V.

ΣΩ. Ἀρ᾽ οὖν μοι, ὦ θαυμάσιε Εὐθύφρον, κράτιστον
ἐστι μαθητῇ σῷ γενέσθαι καὶ πρὸ τῆς γραφῆς τῆς
πρὸς Μέλητον αὐτὰ ταῦτα προκαλεῖσθαι αὐτὸν
λέγοντα, ὅτι ἔγωγε καὶ ἐν τῷ ἔμπροσθεν χρόνῳ τὰ
θεῖα περὶ πολλοῦ ἐποιούμην εἰδεναι, καὶ νῦν ἐπειδη
με ἐκεῖνος αὐτοσχεδιάζοντά φησι καὶ καινοτομοῦντα
περὶ τῶν θείων ἐξαμαρτάνειν, μαθητὴς δὴ γέγονα σός·
καὶ εἰ μὲν, ὦ Μέλητε, φαίην ἄν, Εὐθύφρονα ὁμολογεῖς
Ɓ σοφὸν εἶναι τὰ τοιαῦτα καὶ ὀρθῶς νομίζειν, καὶ ἐμὲ
ἡγοῦ καὶ μὴ δικάζου· εἰ δὲ μή, ἐκείνῳ τῷ διδασκάλῳ
λάχε δίκην πρότερον ἢ ἐμοί, ὡς τοὺς πρεσβυτέρους
διαφθείροντι, ἐμέ τε καὶ τὸν αὐτοῦ πατέρα, ἐμὲ μὲν
διδάσκοντι, ἐκεῖνον δὲ νουθετοῦντί τε καὶ κολάζοντι·

Ἀρ᾽ οὖν, nonne? But acc. to
Hermann it is a milder, less
positive, interrogation than ἀρ᾽
οὖν οὐ.

προκαλεῖσθαι. Like many
verbs in Greek and Latin with
two accusatives. Others are
ἐρωτᾶν, αἰτεῖν, διδάσκειν, ἐννύναι,
ἀφαιρεῖν; and to take another
example of this verb, ἅπερ καὶ
τὸ πρότερον ἤδη προυκαλεσάμεθα,
Thuc. ii., 72, and below at the
end of this passage, ἃ προὐκαλούμην αὐτόν.

αὐτοσχεδιάζειν. σχεδία is a
raft, or piece of light woodwork,
knocked up for a passing occasion, hence a "makeshift."
Hence the word here means to
speak offhand, for the occasion,
without sufficient grounds. It
is especially applicable, Fischer
remarks, to those orators or
rhetors who would undertake to
speak on any given subject
without notice, making up for

solid information by means of
fine language.

B. σοφὸν εἶναι τὰ τοιαῦτα.
For this construction compare
Xen. Cyr., iii., 3, 9, οἱ στρα-
τιῶται . . . ἐπιστήμονες ἦσαν τὰ
προσήκοντα τῇ ἑαυτῶν ἕκαστος
ὁπλίσει; Æsch. Choe. 21, χοὰς
προπομπός, and at the end of this
Dialogue, σοφὸς τὰ θεῖα γέγονα.

τῷ διδασκάλῳ λάχε δ. This
dative is that of the remoter
object, that is the person or
thing affected indirectly by the
action of the verb. It may be
called the Dative of Interest, for
under such a notion would fall
a vast number of examples like
the present in Latin and Greek,
e.g. οἱ Πλαταιεῖς λαγχάνουσι
δίκην τοῖς Λακεδαιμονίοις, Dem.
1378, ii., and αὐτῷ τε Καμβύσῃ
ἐσελθεῖν οἰκτόν τινα, Her. 3, 14.
What is called Dative of Grati-
fication we should put under
this head.

καὶ ἐὰν μή μοι πείθηται μηδ' ἀφίῃ τῆς δίκης ἢ ἀντ'
ἐμοῦ γράφηται σέ, αὐτὰ ταῦτα λέγειν ἐν τῷ δικαστηρίῳ ἃ προὐκαλούμην αὐτόν.

ΕΥΘ. Ναὶ μὰ Δί' ὦ Σώκρατες, εἰ ἄρα ἐμὲ ἐπι-
χειρήσειε γράφεσθαι, εὕροιμ' ἄν, ὡς οἶμαι, ὅπῃ σαθρός C
ἐστι, καὶ πολὺ ἂν ἡμῖν πρότερον περὶ ἐκείνου λόγος
γένοιτο ἐν τῷ δικαστηρίῳ ἢ περὶ ἐμοῦ.

ΣΩ. Καὶ ἐγώ τοι, ὦ φίλε ἑταῖρε, ταῦτα γιγνώσκων
μαθητὴς ἐπιθυμῶ γενέσθαι σός, εἰδὼς ὅτι καὶ ἄλλος
πού τις καὶ ὁ Μέλητος οὗτος σὲ μὲν οὐδὲ δοκεῖ ὁρᾶν,
ἐμὲ δὲ οὕτως ὀξέως ἀτεχνῶς καὶ ῥᾳδίως κατεῖδεν, ὥστε
ἀσεβείας ἐγράψατο. νῦν οὖν πρὸς Διὸς λέγε μοι, ὃ
νῦν δὴ σαφῶς εἰδέναι διισχυρίζου· ποῖόν τι τὸ εὐσεβὲς D

ἀφίῃ. Notice this is not an
intransitive use. με must be
supplied from μοι.

αὐτὰ ταῦτα λέγειν. The construction,which had become quite
a direct one after its introduction by ὅτι, ὅτι ἔγωγε, &c.,
now changes back to the infinitive,
depending really upon κράτιστόν
ἐστι,at the beginning of Socrates'
remarks, as μαθητῇ σῷ γενέσθαι
did before.

ἃ προὐκ. αὐτόν. For this construction, V.S. The object and
effect of this supposed case which
Socrates puts forward is to exhibit Euthyphro in the light of
the reference and authority upon
such questions of religion and
morals as are being discussed
between the two. Euthyphro
takes the bait eagerly. He is
quite ready to help Socrates if
he is in a difficulty, and does not
profess a doubt as to whether he
himself can be mistaken, even
though an Athenian audience
laughs at him. His entire self-
confidence shows amusingly,

contrasted with the insinuating
and humble professions of Socrates, who will learn anything
he can from the omniscient
Euthyphro. This is the εἰρωνεία
of Socrates, where he causes his
companion to believe himself
well-informed, whilst he really
is not.

C. σαθρός, "unsound."
κατεῖδεν—more than εἶδεν,
"see through." So Teiresias
to Oedipus—

ὀργὴν ἐμέμψω τὴν ἐμὴν, τήν
σοι δ' ὁμοῦ
ναίουσαν οὐ κατεῖδες.
SOPH. O. T. 337.

διισχυρίζου σαφῶς εἰδέναι. Cf.
Phaed. 114 D., τὸ μὲν οὖν ταῦτα
διισχυρίσασθαι οὕτως ἔχειν . . .
οὐ πρέπει νοῦν ἔχοντι. For the
fact, V.S. 4, E., init. ad fin.

D. ποῖόν τι. The force of τι
here,though untranslatable, is to
imply ignorance, or an unde-
fined notion in the inquirer's
mind.

φῂς εἶναι καὶ τὸ ἀσεβὲς καὶ περὶ φόνου καὶ περὶ τῶν
ἄλλων; ἢ οὐ ταὐτόν ἐστιν ἐν πάσῃ πράξει τὸ ὅσιον
αὐτὸ αὑτῷ, καὶ τὸ ἀνόσιον αὖ τοῦ μὲν ὁσίου
παντὸς ἐναντίον, αὐτὸ δὲ αὑτῷ ὅμοιον καὶ ἔχον μίαν
τινὰ ἰδέαν κατὰ τὴν ἀνοσιότητα πᾶν, ὅ τί περ ἂν
μέλλῃ ἀνόσιον εἶναι;

ΕΥΘ. Πάντως δήπου, ὦ Σώκρατες.

CAP. VI.

ΣΩ. Λέγε δή, τί φῂς εἶναι τὸ ὅσιον καὶ τί τὸ
ἀνόσιον;

ΕΥΘ. Λέγω τοίνυν, ὅτι τὸ μὲν ὅσιόν ἐστιν ὅπερ
ἐγὼ νῦν ποιῶ, τῷ ἀδικοῦντι ἢ περὶ φόνους ἢ περὶ
ἱερῶν κλοπὰς ἤ τι ἄλλο τῶν τοιούτων ἐξαμαρτάνοντι
Ε ἐπεξιέναι, ἐάν τε πατὴρ ὢν τυγχάνῃ ἐάν τε μήτηρ ἐάν
τε ἄλλος ὁστισοῦν, τὸ δὲ μὴ ἐπεξιέναι ἀνόσιον. ἐπεί,
ὦ Σώκρατες, θέασαι, ὡς μέγα σοι ἐρῶ τεκμήριον τοῦ

ἢ οὐ; nonne?
καὶ τὸ ἀνόσιον αὖ, &c.,
"whilst the impious, *again*, is
that which is contrary to all
that is pious, but is still itself
like itself . . ."
τινὰ, the indefinite again. Although Socrates postulates one
form (ἰδέαν) for the impious, he
purposely avoids defining it—
"Some form or other which is
one."
κατὰ τὴν ἀνος. "according
to," *i.e.* "in virtue of its impiety." πᾶν must thus be taken
with αὐτό, although placed at
the end of the clause for the
sake of rendering clearer the

dependence of the relative
clause ὅτι, &c.
Λέγω τοίνυν. Euthyphro here
makes an error. Socrates asks
in effect, "What is your definition of piety and impiety?"
This requires a *general* description or rule whereby we may
know the one by the other;
but Euthyphro only gives a
special or particular instance or
two, quite inadequate for the
definition Socrates requires. He
says, "This and that is impiety,"
whilst his answer should be
couched in the form, "Piety
consists in . . ."

νόμου ὅτι οὕτως ἔχει, ὃ καὶ ἄλλοις ἤδη εἶπον, ὅτι
ταῦτα ὀρθῶς ἂν εἴη οὕτω γιγνόμενα, μὴ ἐπιτρέπειν
τῷ ἀσεβοῦντι μηδ' ἂν ὁστισοῦν τυγχάνῃ ὤν. αὐτοὶ
γὰρ οἱ ἄνθρωποι τυγχάνουσι νομίζοντες τὸν Δία τῶν
θεῶν ἄριστον καὶ δικαιότατον, καὶ τοῦτον ὁμολογοῦσι
τὸν αὑτοῦ πατέρα δῆσαι, ὅτι τοὺς υἱεῖς κατέπιεν οὐκ C
ἐν δίκῃ, κἀκεῖνόν γε αὖ τὸν αὑτοῦ πατέρα ἐκτεμεῖν
δι' ἕτερα τοιαῦτα· ἐμοὶ δὲ χαλεπαίνουσιν, ὅτι τῷ
πατρὶ ἐπεξέρχομαι ἀδικοῦντι, καὶ οὕτως αὐτοὶ αὑτοῖς
τὰ ἐναντία λέγουσι περί τε τῶν θεῶν καὶ περὶ
ἐμοῦ.

ΣΩ. Ἆρά γε, ὦ Εὐθύφρον, τοῦτ' ἐστίν οὗ ἕνεκα
τὴν γραφὴν φεύγω, ὅτι τὰ τοιαῦτα ἐπειδάν τις περὶ
τῶν θεῶν λέγῃ, δυσχερῶς πως ἀποδέχομαι; δι' ἃ δή,
ὡς ἔοικε, φήσει τίς με ἐξαμαρτάνειν. νῦν οὖν εἰ καὶ
σοὶ ταῦτα ξυνδοκεῖ τῷ εὖ εἰδότι περὶ τῶν τοιούτων,
ἀνάγκη δὴ, ὡς ἔοικε, καὶ ἡμῖν ξυγχωρεῖν. τί γὰρ καὶ B
φήσομεν, οἵ γε καὶ αὐτοὶ ὁμολογοῦμεν περὶ αὐτῶν
μηδὲν εἰδέναι; ἀλλά μοι εἰπὲ πρὸς Φιλίου, σὺ ὡς
ἀληθῶς ἡγεῖ ταῦτα οὕτω γεγονέναι;

E. τοῦ νόμου ὅτι, for ὅτι ὁ
νόμος οὕτως ἔχει. Anglicè, "a
proof of the law being so."
ὅτι ταῦτα, &c., "that this
would be the right course to
take."
ἐπιτρέπειν, "to give in." Cf.
Her. 2, 120, τόν οὐ προσῆκε
ἀδικέοντι τῷ ἀδελφέῳ ἐπιτρέπειν.
αὐτὸν γάρ, &c. Stallb. compares for this story Ar. Nub.
903, πῶς δῆτα δίκης οὔσης ὁ Ζεύς
οὐκ ἀπόλωλεν, τὸν πατέρ' αὑτοῦ
δήσας;
αὐτοὶ αὑτοῖς τὰ ἐν. λεγ.
"They contradict themselves,"
or "stultify themselves."

ἀρά γε τοῦτ' ἐστ. V. S. 5,
init., a speculative, suggestive
interrogation. So Jowett, "May
not this be?" Stallb. wishes to
make it a confident question,
giving confirmatory power to
γε; but this view hardly suits
Socrates' humble approaches to
the wisdom of Euthyphro.
B. ἀνάγκη δή, "THEN I must
give in." Notice the change to
the plural in the pronoun. Stallb.
finds in it a humble self-relega-
tion of Socrates to the mass, or
vulgar.
Φιλίου, i.e. Ζεὺς φίλιος. Cf.
Ar. Ach. 730. Ναὶ τὸν Φίλιον.

D

ΕΥΘ. Καὶ ἔτι γε τούτων θαυμασιώτερα, ὦ Σώκρατες, ἃ οἱ πολλοὶ οὐκ ἴσασι.

ΣΩ. Καὶ πόλεμον ἄρα ἡγεῖ σὺ εἶναι τῷ ὄντι ἐν τοῖς θεοῖς πρὸς ἀλλήλους, καὶ ἔχθρας γε δεινὰς καὶ μάχας καὶ ἄλλα τοιαῦτα πολλά, οἷα λέγεταί τε ὑπὸ τῶν ποιητῶν, καὶ ὑπὸ τῶν ἀγαθῶν γραφέων τά τε ἄλλα ἱερὰ ἡμῖν καταπεποίκιλται, καὶ δὴ καὶ τοῖς μεγάλοις Παναθηναίοις ὁ πέπλος μεστὸς τῶν τοιούτων ποικιλμάτων ἀνάγεται εἰς τὴν ἀκρόπολιν; ταῦτ᾽ ἀληθῆ φῶμεν εἶναι, ὦ Εὐθύφρον;

ΕΥΘ. Μὴ μόνα γε, ὦ Σώκρατες· ἀλλ᾽ ὅπερ ἄρτι εἶπον, καὶ ἄλλα σοι ἐγὼ πολλά, ἐάνπερ βούλῃ, περὶ τῶν θείων διηγήσομαι, ἃ σὺ ἀκούων εὖ οἶδ᾽ ὅτι ἐκπλαγήσει.

καὶ ἔτι. Again an ellipse of the direct reply. V. S. 4, fin. οὐδὲν γάρ. Translate here, "Certainly, and besides these."

καὶ πόλεμον, &c. The point of this inquiry is to elicit from Euthyphro the admission that the gods dispute among themselves, and if so, what becomes of our ultimate authority for right and wrong, if it is variable, not fixed? In the Republic Socrates comes to a conclusion on this point, viz. that all these stories, representing the gods as either vicious or variable, are entirely wrong, and such stories are accordingly banished from his ideal state. Cf. Rep. 378, a very similar passage to this.

καὶ ὑπό, a break in the construction. Transl., "And the devices with which (οἵοις if the construction were regular) our other sacred objects are adorned, notably the robe (which) is devoted to Minerva." We should expect some verb like καταπεποικ. after πέπλος, but we are again surprised. The notion of adornment is put in apposition, viz., μεστὸς τῶν τοιούτ. ποικιλμάτων, and the place of the verb taken by the notion of offering, ἀνάγεται.

C. εὖ οἶδ᾽ ὅτι. A colloquialism; it is equal in value to an asseverative adverb, and like an adverb can be applied to any word in the sentence, e.g. Soph. Ant. 276, πάρειμι γ᾽ ἀκών οὐχ ἔκουσιν, οἶδ᾽ ὅτι. So δηλόνοτι, ch. 7, E, fin. infra.

CAP. VII.

ΣΩ. Οὐκ ἄν θαυμάζοιμι. ἀλλὰ ταῦτα μέν μοι εἰσαῦθις ἐπὶ σχολῆς διηγήσει. νυνὶ δέ, ὅπερ ἄρτι σε ἠρόμην, πειρῶ σαφέστερον εἰπεῖν. οὐ γάρ με, ὦ ἑταῖρε, τὸ πρότερον ἱκανῶς ἐδίδαξας ἐρωτήσαντα τὸ D ὅσιον, ὅ τί ποτ᾽ εἴη, ἀλλά μοι εἶπες, ὅτι τοῦτο τυγχάνει ὅσιον ὄν, ὃ σὺ νῦν ποιεῖς, φόνου ἐπεξιὼν τῷ πατρί.

ΕΥΘ. Καὶ ἀληθῆ γε ἔλεγον, ὦ Σώκρατες.

ΣΩ. Ἴσως. ἀλλὰ γάρ, ὦ Εὐθύφρον, καὶ ἄλλα πολλὰ φῂς εἶναι ὅσια.

ΕΥΘ. Καὶ γὰρ ἔστιν.

ΣΩ. Μέμνησαι οὖν, ὅτι οὐ τοῦτό σοι διεκελευόμην, ἕν τι ἢ δύο με διδάξαι τῶν πολλῶν ὁσίων, ἀλλ᾽ ἐκεῖνο αὐτὸ τὸ εἶδος, ᾧ πάντα τὰ ὅσια ὅσιά ἐστιν; ἔφησθα

D. ὅ τί ποτ᾽ εἴη, V. S. note on λέγω τοίνυν. Here Socrates makes the objection there mentioned. "What impiety was generally (ποτε), was my question, but you tell me that this or that (particular case) is impious, which does not help me to a canon of piety and impiety." καὶ ἀληθῆ. Here Euthyphro misses Socrates' point altogether. Socrates has therefore to bring home the difference between universal and particular by another method. εἶδος. The best explanation of this term is to be found in the words following :—" By virtue of which impiety is impiety." In other words, that quality or mode of action which makes a word or deed impious, without

which it would not be impious, which is common to and will be found in all impiety. The expression, ᾧ πάντα ὅσια ὅσιά ἐστιν corresponds to the expression κατὰ τὴν ἀνοσιοτῆτα, in ch. 5, D. fin., "Having one form in virtue of its impiety," i.e. presenting the same marks or characteristics of impiety by which it is known for impiety. This εἶδος was in Plato's belief a real, existing essence, the universal, whilst particular manifestations of it only existed in an inferior and unreal sense. From which it may be gathered that he looked upon our world and all that it contained as only "the shadow of things perfect." Cf. "Who serve unto the example and shadow of heavenly things."

Ε γάρ που μιᾷ ἰδέᾳ τα τε ἀνόσια ανοσια εἶναι καὶ τὰ ὅσια ὅσια· ἢ οὐ μνημονεύεις ;

ΕΥΘ. Ἔγωγε.

ΣΩ. Ταύτην τοίνυν με αὐτὴν δίδαξον τὴν ἰδέαν, τίς ποτέ ἐστιν, ἵνα εἰς ἐκείνην ἀποβλέπων καὶ χρώμενος αὐτῇ παραδείγματι, ὃ μεν ἄν τοιοῦτον ᾖ, ὧν ἂν ἢ σὺ ἢ ἄλλος τις πράττῃ, φῶ ὅσιον εἶναι, ὃ δ' ἂν μὴ τοιοῦτον, μὴ φῶ.

ΕΥΘ. Ἀλλ' εἰ οὕτω βούλει, ὦ Σώκρατες, και οὕτω σοι φράσω.

ΣΩ. Ἀλλὰ μὴν βούλομαί γε.

ΕΥΘ. Ἔστι τοίνυν τὸ μὲν τοῖς θεοῖς προσφιλὲς ὅσιον, τὸ δὲ μὴ προσφιλὲς ἀνόσιον.

7 ΣΩ. Παγκάλως, ὦ Εὐθύφρον, καὶ ὡς ἐγὼ ἐζήτουν

ἔφησθα γάρ που. An example of Socrates' insinuating use of dialectic. Euthyphro had not actually made this statement. It had been made for him, and put in his mouth by Socrates, V. S. 5 fin., ἔχον μίαν τινὰ ἰδέαν κατὰ τὴν ἀνοσιοτῆτα.

E. Μιᾷ ἰδέα. Notice where this is tending. It has been granted that the gods dispute, and that therefore right and wrong are not fixed, unvariable ; but now we are showing that they are fixed, one, and unalterable.

παραδείγματι. So in Republic, τούτῳ παραδείγματι χρώμενος, where παραδ. is *complement* to τούτῳ, in apposition to it.

Ἔστι τοίνυν. Here Socrates has succeeded in eliciting a general definition of piety and impiety from Euthyphro ; whether it is a right one or a wrong one, he says, remains to be seen. It will easily appear

that we are at once involved in a contradiction by this definition. Thus—

The pious is that which pleases the gods.

But the gods differ.

∴ That which pleases one god displeases another.

Again, the impious is that which displeases the gods.

∴ The same thing can be pious and impious at the same time.

This contradiction he now proceeds to draw out.

ἀλλὰ μὴν . . . "Why of course I want to hear." γε implying, "how can you ask?"

θεοῖς προσφιλές. It will be noticed that the weak point in this definition, apart from the dilemma about the gods' disputes, is that it presupposes an intimate knowledge of the divine nature unknowable to men. As a definition, therefore, it is of no use.

ἀποκρίνασθαι σε, οὕτω νῦν ἀπεκρίνω. εἰ μέντοι ἀληθές, τοῦτο οὔπω οἶδα, ἀλλὰ σὺ δῆλον ὅτι ἐπεκδιδάξεις ὡς ἔστιν ἀληθῆ ἃ λεγεις.

ΕΥΘ. Πάνυ μεν οὖν.

CAP. VIII.

ΣΩ. Φέρε δη, ἐπισκεψώμεθα, τί λέγομεν. τὸ μὲν θεοφιλές τε καὶ ὁ θεοφιλὴς ἄνθρωπος ὅσιος, τὸ δὲ θεομισὲς καὶ ὁ θεομισὴς ἀνόσιος· οὐ ταὐτὸν δ' ἐστὶν, ἀλλὰ τὸ ἐναντιωτατον τὸ ὅσιον τῷ ἀνοσίῳ. οὐχ οὕτως;

ΕΥΘ. Οὕτω μὲν οὖν.

ΣΩ. Καὶ εὖ γε φαίνεται εἰρῆσθαι.

ΕΥΘ. Δοκῶ, ὦ Σώκρατες· εἴρηται γάρ. B

ΣΩ. Οὐκοῦν καὶ ὅτι στασιάζουσιν οἱ θεοί, ὦ Εὐθύφρον, καὶ διαφέρονται ἀλλήλοις καὶ ἔχθρα ἐστὶν ἐν αὐτοῖς πρὸς ἀλλήλους, καὶ τοῦτο εἴρηται;

ΕΥΘ. Εἴρηται γάρ.

ΣΩ. Ἔχθραν δὲ καὶ ὀργάς, ὦ ἄριστε, ἡ περί τίνων διαφορὰ ποιεῖ; ὧδε δὲ σκοπῶμεν. ἆρ' ἂν εἰ

δῆλον ὅτι. V.S. on εὖ οἶδ' ὅτι.
B. Δοκῶ, censeo. This personal use is not infrequent. Cf. Soph. 221, A., δοκῶ μὲν, ὅπερ ἄρτι προὐθέμεθα δεῖν ἐξευρεῖν, τοῦτ' αὐτὸ νῦν ἀποτετελέσθαι. In 12 init. we have, Ἐγωγέ μοι δοκῶ μανθάνειν; where the constructions meet halfway.
εἴρηται γάρ . . . In 5 fin. καὶ τὸ ἀνόσιον αὖ τοῦ μὲν ὁσίου παντὸς ἐναντίον. Euthyphro seems to hint, "As if there could be any doubt about what I have given my assent to!"
ἡ περὶ τίνων διαφορά. . . . "What is the dispute, and about what do they differ?"
ἆρ' ἂν εἰ. We get ἂν thus early in the sentence to show

that it is to be a potential one, a contingency. So οὐκ οἶδ' ἂν εἰ πείσαιμι, Eur. Med. 941, where the potential particle ἂν, as in the present passage, qualifies the verb. So in Timaeus 26 B., οὐκ ἂν οἶδα εἰ δυναίμην ἅπαντα ἐν μνήμῃ πάλιν λαβεῖν; where ἂν must be taken with δυναίμην.
περὶ ἀριθμοῦ, "about number," i.e. "in a question of numbers." In this example Socrates is leading up to the principle, that questions on which we should differ would be the abstruse and complex problems of morals, religion, &c. Hence the differences of the gods must be also concerning the most important and radical principles.

διαφεροίμεθα ἐγώ τε καὶ σὺ περὶ ἀριθμοῦ, ὁπότερα
πλείω, ἡ περὶ τούτων διαφορὰ ἐχθροὺς ἂν ἡμᾶς
C ποιοῖ καὶ ὀργίζεσθαι ἀλλήλοις, ἢ ἐπὶ λογισμὸν ἐλθόντες περί γε τῶν τοιούτων ταχὺ ἂν ἀπαλλα-
γεῖμεν;
ΕΥΘ. Πάνυ γε.
ΣΩ. Οὐκοῦν καὶ περὶ τοῦ μείζονος καὶ ἐλάττο-
νος εἰ διαφεροίμεθα, ἐπὶ τὸ μετρεῖν ἐλθόντες ταχὺ
παυσαίμεθ' ἂν τῆς διαφορᾶς;
ΕΥΘ. Ἔστι ταῦτα.
ΣΩ. Καὶ ἐπί γε τὸ ἱστάναι ἐλθόντες, ὡς ἐγᾦμαι,
περὶ τοῦ βαρυτέρου τε καὶ κουφοτέρου διακριθεῖμεν
ἄν;
ΕΥΘ. Πῶς γὰρ οὔ;
ΣΩ. Περὶ τίνος δὲ δὴ διενεχθέντες καὶ ἐπὶ τίνα
κρίσιν οὐ δυνάμενοι ἀφικέσθαι ἐχθροί γε ἂν ἀλλήλοις εἶμεν καὶ ὀργιζοίμεθα; ἴσως οὐ πρόχειρόν σοί
D ἐστιν, ἀλλ' ἐμοῦ λέγοντος σκόπει, εἰ τάδ' ἐστὶ τό τε
δίκαιον καὶ τὸ ἄδικον καὶ καλὸν καὶ αἰσχρὸν καὶ
ἀγαθὸν καὶ κακόν. ἆρ' οὐ ταῦτά ἐστι, περὶ ὧν διενεχθέντες καὶ οὐ δυνάμενοι ἐπὶ ἱκανὴν κρίσιν αὐτῶν
ἐλθεῖν ἐχθροὶ ἀλλήλοις γιγνόμεθα, ὅταν γιγνώμεθα,
καὶ ἐγὼ καὶ σὺ καὶ οἱ ἄλλοι ἄνθρωποι πάντες;
ΕΥΘ. Ἀλλ' ἔστιν αὕτη ἡ διαφορά, ὦ Σώκρατες,
καὶ περὶ τούτων.

C. περί γε τῶν τ. "In (trivial)
matters of this sort."
ἱστάναι, "weighing," lit.
"standing" (act.) i.e. "poising,"
"producing an equilibrium."
Hence the name of statics,
which is the consideration of
bodies in equilibrium.
ἐπὶ τίνα κρίσιν; "to what
tribunal?"

D. τάδ', "these (subjects of
dispute)."
γιγνόμεθα. A touch of realism
in the middle of an imaginary
situation. We should have expected γιγνοίμεθα ἂν. As the
sentence goes on, we see how the
transition takes place in the writer's mind, with the words, καὶ
ἐγὼ καὶ σὺ καὶ πάντες ἄνθρωποι.

ΣΩ. Τί δέ; οἱ θεοί, ὦ Εὐθύφρον, οὐκ. εἴπερ τις διαφέρονται, δι' αὐτὰ ταῦτα διαφεροιντ' ἄν;

ΕΥΘ. Πολλὴ ἀνάγκη.

ΣΩ. Καὶ τῶν θεῶν ἄρα, ὦ γενναῖε Εὐθύφρον, Ε ἄλλοι ἄλλα δίκαια ἡγοῦνται κατὰ τὸν σὸν λόγον, καὶ καλὰ καὶ αἰσχρὰ καὶ ἀγαθὰ καὶ κακά. οὐ γὰρ ἄν που ἐστασίαζον ἀλλήλοις, εἰ μὴ περὶ τούτων διεφέροντο· ἢ γάρ;

ΕΥΘ. Ὀρθῶς λέγεις.

ΣΩ. Οὐκοῦν ἅπερ καλὰ ἡγοῦνται ἕκαστοι καὶ ἀγαθὰ καὶ δίκαια, ταῦτα καὶ φιλοῦσι, τὰ δὲ ἐναντία τούτων μισοῦσιν;

ΕΥΘ. Πάνυ γε.

ΣΩ. Ταὐτὰ δέ γε, ὡς σὺ φῄς, οἱ μὲν δίκαια ἡγοῦνται, οἱ δὲ ἄδικα· περὶ ἃ καὶ ἀμφισβητοῦντες στασιάζουσί τε καὶ πολεμοῦσιν ἀλλήλοις. ἆρ' οὐχ οὕτως; 8

ΕΥΘ. Οὕτως.

ΣΩ. Ταὐτὰ ἄρα, ὡς ἔοικε, μισεῖταί τε ὑπὸ τῶν θεῶν καὶ φιλεῖται, καὶ θεομισῆ τε καὶ θεοφιλῆ ταῦτ' ἂν εἴη.

ΕΥΘ. Ἔοικεν.

ΣΩ. Καὶ ὅσια ἄρα καὶ ἀνόσια τὰ αὐτὰ ἂν εἴη, ω Εὐθύφρον, τούτῳ τῷ λόγῳ.

ΕΥΘ. Κινδυνεύει.

τί δέ introduces a new step in the argument. "What then?" δι' αὐτὰ τ., "through," i.e. "on account of," "in our desire to settle such matters as these." E. οὐ γάρ, &c. That is, "these are the only subjects upon which we can possibly imagine them differing—the highest and most complex questions." ἄλλα, predicate.

ταὐτὰ. Notice accent. τούτῳ τῷ λόγῳ. Dativus Modi. Similar examples are τούτῳ τρόπῳ, πλήθει πολλοί. In Latin by a preposition or-ablative, e.g., secundum tuum sermonem. Hoc modo. κινδυνεύει. It will be well here to review the last section of the Dialogue, which ends at this point. Socrates had asked (cap.

CAP. IX.

ΣΩ. Οὐκ ἄρα ὃ ἠρόμην ἀπεκρίνω, ὦ θαυμάσιε. οὐ γὰρ τοῦτό γε ἠρώτων, ὃ τυγχάνει ταὐτὸν ὂν ὅσιόν τε καὶ ἀνόσιον· ὃ δ᾽ ἂν θεοφιλὲς ᾖ, καὶ θεομισές ἐστιν, ὡς ἔοικεν. ὥστε, ὦ Εὐθύφρον, ὃ σὺ νῦν ποιεῖς τὸν πατέρα κολάζων, οὐδὲν θαυμαστόν, εἰ τοῦτο δρῶν τῷ μὲν Διὶ προσφιλὲς ποιεῖς, τῷ δὲ Κρόνῳ καὶ τῷ Οὐρανῷ ἐχθρόν, καὶ τῷ μὲν Ἡφαίστῳ φίλον, τῇ δὲ Ἥρᾳ ἐχθρόν· καὶ εἴ τις ἄλλος τῶν θεῶν ἕτερος ἑτέρῳ διαφέρεται περὶ αὐτοῦ, καὶ ἐκείνοις κατὰ ταὐτά.

ΕΥΘ. Ἀλλ᾽ οἶμαι, ὦ Σώκρατες, περί γε τούτου τῶν θεῶν οὐδένα ἕτερον ἑτέρῳ διαφέρεσθαι, ὡς οὐ δεῖ δίκην διδόναι ἐκεῖνον, ὃς ἂν ἀδίκως τινὰ ἀποκτείνῃ.

7 init.) for a general definition of the pious and impious. Euthyphro's definition had been, "That which the gods love is pious; that which they hate is impious." "But," replies Socrates, "you have already allowed that they are not at one with each other on many subjects, and, if so, they will certainly dispute on this one we are considering. Therefore if one god loves the same thing which another hates, your definition will not hold."

ὃ δ᾽ ἂν θεοφ... "But whatever is beloved of heaven, that is also hated of heaven." Notice conjunctive and indicative senses.

B. τῷ μὲν Διί... For Zeus had set the example of ill-using parents, whilst Cronus and Uranus had been both of them sufferers, and Hephaestus had been expelled by his father from heaven.

καὶ ἐκείνοις κατὰ ταὐτά. "It will be to them according to the same," i.e. "there will be the same difference in their case as well." For this dative V.S. note on τῷ διδασκάλῳ λάχε δίκην, 5 ad. med. B.

Ἀλλ᾽ οἶμαι. Euthyphro here starts on a wrong scent. "However they may differ" says he, "in other things, they do not differ on this cardinal point, viz., that justice should be done." "No more do men differ on that point," replies Socrates.

ὡς οὐ δεῖ... The οὐ seems redundant to us. But it brings out the differing, the other side of the question to the one usually adopted. It is what the opponent would say. We have οὐ and not μὴ in the dependent sentence because, in the words of Matthiae, the sentence does not express the thought of the speaker (but that of another person), nor has reference to his thought. Or we may look at it merely as the negation of δεῖ, comparing οὐκ ἐῶ, οὔ φημι.

ΣΩ. Τί δέ; ἀνθρώπων, ὦ Εὐθύφρον, ἤδη τινὸς
ἤκουσας ἀμφισβητοῦντος, ὡς τὸν ἀδίκως ἀποκτείναντα C
ἢ ἄλλο ἀδίκως ποιοῦντα ὁτιοῦν οὐ δεῖ δίκην διδόναι;
ΕΥΘ. Οὐδὲν μὲν οὖν παύονται ταῦτ᾽ ἀμφισβητοῦντες καὶ ἄλλοθι καὶ ἐν τοῖς δικαστηρίοις. ἀδι-
κοῦντες γὰρ πάμπολλα, πάντα ποιοῦσι καὶ λέγουσι
φεύγοντες τὴν δίκην.
ΣΩ. Ἦ καὶ ὁμολογοῦσιν, ὦ Εὐθύφρον, ἀδικεῖν,
καὶ ὁμολογοῦντες ὅμως οὐ δεῖν φασὶ σφᾶς διδόναι
δίκην;
ΕΥΘ. Οὐδαμῶς τοῦτό γε.
ΣΩ. Οὐκ ἄρα πᾶν γε ποιοῦσι καὶ λέγουσι. τοῦτο
γάρ, οἶμαι, οὐ τολμῶσι λέγειν οὐδ᾽ ἀμφισβητεῖν, ὡς
οὐχί, εἴπερ ἀδικοῦσί γε, δοτέον δίκην· ἀλλ᾽ οἶμαι, οὔ D
φασιν ἀδικεῖν· ἢ γάρ;
ΕΥΘ. Ἀληθῆ λέγεις.
ΣΩ. Οὐκ ἄρα ἐκεῖνό γε ἀμφισβητοῦσιν, ὡς οὐ τὸν
ἀδικοῦντα δεῖ διδόναι δίκην· ἀλλ᾽ ἐκεῖνο ἴσως ἀμφισβητοῦσι, τὸ τίς ἐστιν ὁ ἀδικῶν καὶ τί δρῶν καὶ
πότε.

C. οὐδὲν μὲν οὖν παύονται.
"On the contrary, they are
always," &c. Cf. Soph. O. C.
30, 31.

OI. ἢ δεῦρο προσστείχοντα κἀξορ-
μώμενον;
AN. καὶ δὴ μὲν οὖν πάροντα.
Oed. On his way towards us?
An. Nay. Just here.

In this reply Euthyphro fails
to see the exact meaning of
Socrates' question. He has not
been asked, "Do men try to get
off punishment?" but "Do men
openly deny that justice must be
done after a crime?" This
Socrates puts more clearly in his
next question.

ἦ καὶ ὁμολ. "Yes, but do
they allow, &c.?" καὶ prefixed
to a word thus often implies a
belief .in the speaker that the
thing is not so; V.S. ch. 2, init.
τί καὶ ποιοῦντά σέ φησι διαφθείρειν τοὺς νέους;
οὐκ ἄρα. "The difficulty is
to get them to acknowledge
themselves in the wrong.
D. τὸ τίς, &c. A good ex-
ample of a whole sentence, containing two or three clauses,
becoming a noun substantive
and being manipulated as such.
Cf. Plat. Rep. 327. οὐκοῦν, ἦν
δ᾽ ἐγώ, ἐν ἔτι λείπεται τὸ ἢν πεί-
σωμεν ὑμᾶς, ὡς χρὴ ἡμᾶς ἀφεῖναι.
Here we have the difficulty stated

ΕΥΘ. Ἀληθῆ λέγεις.

ΣΩ. Οὐκοῦν αὐτά γε ταῦτα καὶ οἱ θεοὶ πεπόν-
θασιν, εἴπερ στασιάζουσι περὶ τῶν δικαίων καὶ
ἀδίκων, ὡς ὁ σὸς λόγος, καὶ οἱ μέν φασιν ἀλλήλους
ἀδικεῖν, οἱ δὲ οὔ φασιν; ἐπεὶ ἐκεῖνό γε δήπου, ὦ
θαυμάσιε, οὐδεὶς οὔτε θεῶν οὔτε ἀνθρώπων τολμᾷ
Ε λέγειν, ὡς οὐ τῷ γε ἀδικοῦντι δοτέον δίκην.

ΕΥΘ. Ναί, τοῦτο μὲν ἀληθὲς λέγεις, ὦ Σώκρατες,
τό γε κεφάλαιον.

ΣΩ. Ἀλλ᾽ ἕκαστόν γε, οἶμαι, ὦ Εὐθύφρον, τῶν
πραχθέντων ἀμφισβητοῦσιν οἱ ἀμφισβητοῦντες, καὶ
ἄνθρωποι καὶ θεοί, εἴπερ ἀμφισβητοῦσι θεοί· πράξεώς
τινος πέρι διαφερόμενοι οἱ μὲν δικαίως φασὶν αὐτὴν
πεπρᾶχθαι, οἱ δὲ ἀδίκως· ἆρ᾽ οὐχ οὕτως;

ΕΥΘ. Πάνυ γε.

in definite language. "Men are ready enough to do justice when they know what it is, especially in its special cases, what and where and when. The difficulty is to know these points."

οὐκοῦν, &c. "Is it not then the same case exactly with the gods too?" Lit. "Do not the gods experience this?" Cf. Rep. 563, C., αὐτὸς γὰρ εἰς ἀγρὸν πορευόμενος θαμὰ αὐτὸ πάσχω. ὡς ὁ σὸς λόγος. Again, Euthyphro had only had this admission extorted from him. V. S. 8, D.

οὔ φασιν, "negant," i.e. nec—aiunt.

E. τῷ γε ἀδικοῦντι. Dative of interest; the person concerned in the δίκης δόσις. V. S. note on 5 B. ad med.

τό γε κεφάλαιον. Jelf describes this as an accusative in apposition; but it is hard to help looking upon it in some passages as a nom., e.g. Theat. 190, B., ἢ καί, τὸ πάντων κεφάλαιον, σκοπεῖ εἴ ποτ᾽, &c. Here, no doubt, the accusatival sense suits better, like such expressions as ἐπὶ δὲ στενάχοντο γυναῖκες Πάτροκλον πρόφασιν, σφῶν δ᾽ αὐτῶν κήδε᾽ ἑκάστη.

ἕκαστον. Not "every particular," but a "particular case," or "particulars," explained further on by πράξεώς τινος.

CAP. X.

ΣΩ. Ἴθι τοίνυν, ὦ φίλε Εὐθύφρον, δίδαξον καὶ 9
ἐμέ, ἵνα σοφώτερος γένωμαι, τί σοι τεκμήριόν ἐστιν,
ὡς παντες θεοὶ ἡγοῦνται ἐκεῖνον ἀδίκως τεθνάναι, ὃς
ἂν θητεύων ἀνδροφόνος γενόμενος, ξυνδεθεὶς ὑπὸ τοῦ
δεσπότου τοῦ ἀποθανόντος, φθάσῃ τελευτήσας διὰ τὰ
δεσμά, πρὶν τὸν ξυνδήσαντα παρὰ τῶν ἐξηγητῶν περὶ
αὐτοῦ πυθέσθαι, τί χρὴ ποιεῖν, καὶ ὑπὲρ τοῦ τοιούτου
δὴ ὀρθῶς ἔχει ἐπεξιέναι καὶ ἐπισκήπτεσθαι φόνου τὸν
υἱὸν τῷ πατρί· ἴθι, περὶ τούτων πειρῶ τί μοι σαφὲς
ἐνδείξασθαι, ὡς παντὸς μᾶλλον πάντες θεοὶ ἡγοῦνται
ὀρθῶς ἔχειν ταύτην τὴν πρᾶξιν. κἄν μοι ἱκανῶς Β

δίδαξ. Euthyphro being probably discouraged by having his mistake thus plainly set before him, has to be reassured by fresh professions of inferior knowledge on Socrates' part.

ὡς πάντες θεοὶ ἡγοῦνται ... After these words we have a general description of the occurrence, the words καὶ ὑπὲρ τοῦ τοιούτου depending on τί τεκμήριον ἐστιν ὡς: "How do you know that all the gods think... and that it is right?"

ὃς ἂν θητεύων ... φθάσῃ. Socrates puts the case indefinitely, so as to qualify the direct interrogative and soften his apparent incredulity : "Supposing a man to be serving, and were to commit a murder," &c. Hence the employment of the potential ἄν, expressing contingent or possible action, and of the conjunctive. But it is not an entirely imaginary case. Hence the conjunctive is primary.

ἀνδροφόνος γεν. This expression seems to imply possible

innocence of intent to slay. Translate, "committed manslaughter."

φθάσῃ τελευτήσας. Take with πρίν, "loses his life before..." Cf. 4, init., ὅς γε τυγχάνει ὤν εὖ μάλα πρεσβύτης. For this verb, Xen. Cyr. I, 3, 12. χαλεπὸν ἦν ἄλλον φθάσαι τοῦτο ποιήσαντα, sc. "To do this before he did."

δεσμά. Noun heteroclite.

ἐπισκήπτεσθαι. "Dicitur de iis, quae cum impetu quodam in aliquid irruunt." Stallb. Σκήπτω is used of a darting light in Aesch. Ag. 302, λίμνην δ' ὕπερ Γοργῶπιν ἔσκηψεν φάος. For the gen. φόνου, cf. damnatur capitis, and capitis accusare in Nepos.

παντὸς μᾶλλον. The sense of comparison is lost here : "without doubt," "absolutely." Cf. Rep. 555, D., καὶ εἰσδανείζοντες ἔτι πλουσιώτεροι καὶ ἐντιμότεροι γίγνωνται; to which the answer is, παντός γε μᾶλλον

ἐνδείξῃ, ἐγκωμιάζων σε ἐπὶ σοφίᾳ οὐδέποτε παυσομαι.

ΕΥΘ. Ἀλλ᾽ ἴσως οὐκ ὀλίγον ἔργον ἐστίν, ὦ Σώκρατες· ἐπεὶ πάνυ γε σαφῶς ἔχοιμι ἂν ἐπιδεῖξαί σοι.

ΣΩ. Μανθάνω· ὅτι σοι δοκῶ τῶν δικαστῶν δυσμαθέστερος εἶναι· ἐπεὶ ἐκείνοις γε ἐνδείξει δῆλον ὅτι, ὡς ἄδικά τέ ἐστι καὶ οἱ θεοὶ ἅπαντες τὰ τοιαῦτα μισοῦσιν.

ΕΥΘ. Πάνυ γε σαφῶς, ὦ Σώκρατες, ἐάν περ ἀκούωσί γέ μου λέγοντος.

CAP. XI.

C ΣΩ. Ἀλλ᾽ ἀκούσονται, ἐάνπερ εὖ δοκῇς λέγειν. τόδε δὲ σοῦ ἐνενόησα ἅμ λέγοντος, καὶ πρὸς ἐμαυτὸν σκοπῶ· εἰ ὅ τι μάλιστά με Εὐθύφρων διδάξειεν, ὡς οἱ θεοὶ ἅπαντες τὸν τοιοῦτον θάνατον ἡγοῦνται ἄδικον εἶναι, τί μᾶλλον ἐγὼ μεμάθηκα παρ᾽ Εὐθύφρονος, τί ποτ᾽ ἐστὶ τὸ ὅσιόν τε καὶ τὸ ἀνόσιον; θεομισὲς μὲν γὰρ τοῦτο τὸ ἔργον, ὡς ἔοικεν, εἴη ἄν. ἀλλὰ γὰρ οὐ

B. ἐπεί. To this truly mobile particle it is hard to assign a meaning that will serve for more than two consecutive passages. Euthyphro says, " It will likely be a long affair ; " and " I could lay the question before you very clearly." What then is the connection between these two remarks ? If we look on to Socrates' rejoinder it will seem that he takes Euthyphro's remark to imply, "You will need a lot of explanation," and allows that he is certainly very dense. The full sense would then seem to be, " 'Twill be a long business since (you will need it explained very clearly, and this I shall be able, and) feel it my duty to do."

μανθάνω, "I comprehend." Cf. Ar. Birds, 1003, ΜΕ. Μανθάνεις; ΠΕ. Οὐ μανθάνω. Others join μανθάνω ὅτι ...
τῶν δικαστῶν δυσμ. Refers to the words in 3 B., πολὺ ἂν ἡμῖν πρότερον περὶ ἐκείνου λόγος γένοιτο ἐν τῷ δικαστηρίῳ ἤ περὶ ἐμοῦ.
C. τόδε refers to what follows.
Εὐθύφρων. The third person here instead of the second gives an additional weight to the statement of the situation, enabling Euthyphro as it were to put himself outside himself, and view the difficulty as a disinterested spectator.
ὡς ἔοικεν, i.e. according to Euthyphro's decision on ground of his own knowledge.

τούτῳ ἐφάνη ἄρτι ὡρισμένα τὸ ὅσιον καὶ μή. τὸ γὰρ
θεομισὲς ὂν καὶ θεοφιλὲς ἐφάνη. ὥστε τούτου μὲν
ἀφίημί σε, ὦ Εὐθύφρον, καὶ εἰ βούλει, πάντες αὐτὸ D
ἡγείσθωσαν θεοὶ ἄδικον καὶ πάντες μισούντων. ἀλλ᾽
ἆρα τοῦτο νῦν ἐπανορθούμεθα ἐν τῷ λόγῳ ὡς ὃ μὲν
ἂν πάντες οἱ θεοὶ μισῶσιν, ἀνόσιόν ἐστιν, ὃ δ᾽ ἂν
φιλῶσιν, ὅσιον· ὃ δ᾽ ἂν οἱ μὲν φιλῶσιν, οἱ δὲ μισῶσιν,
οὐδέτερα ἢ ἀμφότερα; ἆρ᾽ οὕτω βούλει ἡμῖν ὡρίσθαι
νῦν περὶ τοῦ ὁσίου καὶ τοῦ ἀνοσίου;

ΕΥΘ. Τί γὰρ κωλύει, ὦ Σώκρατες;

ΣΩ. Οὐδὲν ἐμέ γε, ὦ Εὐθύφρον, ἀλλὰ σὺ δὴ τὸ
σὸν σκόπει, εἰ τοῦτο ὑποθέμενος οὕτω ῥᾷστά με
διδάξεις ὃ ὑπέσχου.

ΕΥΘ. Ἀλλ᾽ ἔγωγε φαίην ἂν τοῦτο εἶναι τὸ ὅσιον,
ὃ ἂν πάντες οἱ θεοὶ φιλῶσι, καὶ τὸ ἐναντίον, ὃ ἂν E
πάντες οἱ θεοὶ μισῶσιν, ἀνόσιον.

ΣΩ. Οὐκοῦν ἐπισκοπῶμεν αὖ τοῦτο, ὦ Εὐθύφρον,
εἰ καλῶς λέγεται; ἢ ἐῶμεν καὶ οὕτως ἡμῶν τε αὐτῶν
ἀποδεχώμεθα καὶ τῶν ἄλλων, ἐὰν μόνον φῇ τίς
τι ἔχειν οὕτω, ξυγχωροῦντες ἔχειν; ἢ σκεπτέον, τί
λέγει ὁ λέγων;

ΕΥΘ. Σκεπτέον. οἶμαι μέντοι ἔγωγε τοῦτο νυνὶ
καλῶς λέγεσθαι.

οὐ τούτῳ ἐφ. ἄρτι ὡρ., "These
distinctions have no bearing on
the definition of piety and impiety."—Jowett.

τὸ γὰρ, subj., θεομισὲς ὂν appo-
sitive, καὶ θεοφιλές, predicative.

ἀφίημί σε, "I let you off from
this;" i.e., "You need not con-
cern yourself about proving that
to me."

D. ἐπανορθούμεθα, "set up-
right afresh;" prove and justify
any proposition. Stallb. aptly
compares ἐλέγχειν, which com-
bines the two notions of dis-

proving an antagonist's assertion
and proving your own. Cf. Ar.
Eccl. 485, τὸ πρᾶγμ᾽ ἐλεγχθέν.

ὡς ὃ μέν. The emphatic word
in this sentence is πάντες,
"What all the gods hate."

οὐδέτερα ἢ ἀμφότερα. Cf. Rep.
555, D, οἱ μὲν ὀφείλοντες χρέα,
οἱ δὲ ἄτιμοι γεγονότες, οἱ δὲ
ἀμφότερα. ᾽

Ε. ἡμῶν τε αὐτ. ἀποδεχ . . .
"on our own or other's authority." Cf. Phaed. 92, E., μήτε
ἐμαυτοῦ μήτε ἄλλου ἀποδέ-
χεσθαι.

CAP. XII.

ΣΩ. Τάχ', ὦ 'γαθέ, βέλτιον εἰσόμεθα. ἐννόησον
10 γὰρ τὸ τοιόνδε· ἆρα τὸ ὅσιον, ὅτι ὅσιόν ἐστι, φιλεῖται
ὑπὸ τῶν θεῶν, ἢ ὅτι φιλεῖται, ὅσιόν ἐστιν;
ΕΥΘ. Οὐκ οἶδ' ὅ τι λέγεις, ὦ Σώκρατες.
ΣΩ. Ἀλλ' ἐγὼ πειράσομαι σαφέστερον φράσαι·
λέγομέν τι φερόμενον καὶ φέρον, καὶ ἀγόμενον καὶ
ἄγον, καὶ ὁρώμενον καὶ ὁρῶν· καὶ πάντα τὰ τοιαῦτα μανθάνεις ὅτι ἕτερα ἀλλήλων ἐστὶ καὶ ᾗ ἕτερα.
ΕΥΘ. Ἔγωγέ μοι δοκῶ μανθάνειν.
ΣΩ. Οὐκοῦν καὶ φιλούμενόν τί ἐστι, καὶ τούτου
ἕτερον τὸ φιλοῦν;

Ἄρα τὸ ὅσιον ... In other words, "Are these gods with their quarrels and disputes to be the rule for us, or is there a higher basis or sanction of Right which they recognise in their better moments?"

οὐκ οἶδ' ... Notice Euthyphro's inacquaintance with the logic of the Sophists.

καὶ πάντα, &c. "And that there is a difference in all such things; and where the difference lies."

ᾗ, "in what way, manner, or regard." Cf. Lat. qua.

οὐκοῦν, &c. The drift of this piece of reasoning requires elucidation. In brief it is this : "All things that are in a particular condition are so because they have been brought into it by a motive power, e.g. the carried, the led, the become, the loved, have all had some one to carry, lead, make, or love them. Now Euthyphro and I are asking, Is piety to be defined as 'the loved of the gods?' No. Because we must not say that, because we find the two (viz., piety and the loved of the gods) roughly corresponding, we are to rest satisfied. Piety may be something more than the loved of the gods. And we know that the 'loved of the gods' implies that the gods love. Now the gods loving is prior to loved of the gods. So we can put our definition back a step and say, 'Piety is found in all cases of the gods loving;' and there may be other cases unknown to us of piety. Clearly, then, Piety, or the Holy, is the larger and anterior notion. For 'Heaven loves' is anterior to 'loved of Heaven.' If a reason or cause is to be found for 'Heaven loves,' we are irresistibly forced back to the principle because it is holy." This, then, is the order : (1) This is Holy; (2) Therefore all the gods love it; so we find that (3) Things holy are god-beloved. Thus does Plato deify the Idea, and rationalise the deity, being driven to his conclusion by the state of the popular theology.

ΕΥΘ. Πῶς γὰρ οὔ;

ΣΩ. Λέγε δή μοι, πότερον τὸ φερόμενον, διότι Β φέρεται, φερόμενόν ἐστιν, ἢ δι' ἄλλο τι;

ΕΥΘ. Οὔκ, ἀλλὰ διὰ τοῦτο.

ΣΩ. Καὶ τὸ ἀγόμενον δή, διότι ἄγεται, καὶ τὸ ὁρώμενον, διότι ὁρᾶται;

ΕΥΘ. Πάνυ γε.

ΣΩ. Οὐκ ἄρα διότι ὁρώμενόν γέ ἐστι, διὰ τοῦτο ὁρᾶται, ἀλλὰ τοὐναντίον διότι ὁρᾶται, διὰ τοῦτο ὁρώμενον· οὐδὲ διότι ἀγόμενόν ἐστι, διὰ τοῦτο ἄγεται ἀλλὰ διότι ἄγεται, διὰ τοῦτο ἀγόμενον· οὐδὲ διότι φερόμενον, φέρεται, ἀλλὰ διότι φέρεται, φερόμενον. ἆρα κατάδηλον, ὦ Εὐθύφρον, ὃ βούλομαι λέγειν; βούλομαι δὲ τόδε, ὅτι, εἴ τι γίγνεται ἢ C εἴ τι πάσχει τι, οὐχ ὅτι γιγνόμενόν ἐστι, γίγνεται, ἀλλ' ὅτι γίγνεται, γιγνόμενόν ἐστιν· οὐδ' ὅτι πάσχον ἐστί, πάσχει, ἀλλ' ὅτι πάσχει, πάσχον ἐστίν· ἢ οὐ ξυγχωρεῖς οὕτως;

ΕΥΘ. Ἔγωγε.

ΣΩ. Οὐκοῦν καὶ τὸ φιλούμενον ἢ γιγνόμενόν τί ἐστιν ἢ πάσχον τι ὑπό του;

ΕΥΘ. Πάνυ γε.

ΣΩ. Καὶ τοῦτο ἄρα οὕτως ἔχει, ὥσπερ τὰ προτερα· οὐχ ὅτι φιλούμενόν ἐστι, φιλεῖται ὑπὸ ὧν φιλεῖται, ἀλλ' ὅτι φιλεῖται, φιλούμενον;

ΕΥΘ. Ἀνάγκη.

B. Οὐκ ἄρα, &c. This is to show that the θεοφιλές is not the cause of the gods loving it, but, e contrario, the gods loving is the cause of its being θεοφιλές. It is not therefore holy, because θεοφιλές.

C. βούλομαι λέγειν, "mean." Cf. French "vouloir dire."

Οὐκοῦν . . . "Well, and the loved has become what it is, or is what it is through some agency?"

ὑπὸ ὧν. V. S. note on ὧν προεῖπον, II.

D ΣΩ. Τί δη οὖν λέγομεν περὶ τοῦ ὁσίου, ὦ Εὐθίφρον; ἄλλο τι φιλεῖται ὑπὸ θεῶν παντων, ὡς ὁ σὸς λόγος;

ΕΥΘ. Ναι.

ΣΩ. Ἆρα διὰ τοῦτο, ὅτι ὅσιόν ἐστιν, ἢ δι' ἄλλο τι;

ΕΥΘ. Οὔκ, ἀλλὰ δια τοῦτο.

ΣΩ. Διότι ἄρα ὅσιόν ἐστι, φιλεῖται, ἀλλ' οὐχ ὅτι φιλεῖται, διὰ τοῦτο ὅσιον ἐστιν;

ΕΥΘ. Ἔοικεν.

ΣΩ. Ἀλλὰ μὲν δὴ διοτι γε φιλεῖται ὑπὸ θεῶν, φιλούμενόν ἐστι καὶ θεοφιλὲς τὸ θεοφιλές.

ΕΥΘ. Πῶς γὰρ οὔ;

ΣΩ. Οὐκ ἄρα τὸ θεοφιλὲς ὅσιόν ἐστιν, ὦ Εὐθύφρον, οὐδὲ τὸ ὅσιον θεοφιλές, ὡς σὺ λέγεις, ἀλλ' Ε ἕτερον τοῦτο τουτου.

ΕΥΘ. Πῶς δή, ὦ Σώκρατες;

ΣΩ. Ὅτι ὁμολογοῦμεν τὸ μὲν ὅσιόν διὰ τοῦτο φιλεῖσθαι, ὅτι ὅσιόν ἐστιν, ἀλλ' οὐ διότι φιλεῖται, ὅσιον εἶναι· ἢ γαρ;

ΕΥΩ. Ναί.

D. ἄλλο τι φιλεῖται . . . *i.e.* "We have without doubt agreed that all the gods love it." The whole phrase was ἄλλο τι ἤ. So in Her. 1, 109, ἄλλοτι ἢ λείπεται τὸ ἐνθεῦτεν ἐμοὶ κινδύνων ὁ μέγιστος ;

Διότι ἄρα . . . We here assume the major premise, " Because a thing is holy ∴ it is god-beloved."

Οὐκ ἄρα τὸ θεοφιλές, &c. The god-beloved is not therefore the same thing as the holy, or " The god-beloved and the holy are not coextensive and coincident."

Ε. ὅτι ὁμολογοῦμεν . . . In this chapter Socrates has been proving two propositions :—

(1) That the θεοφιλες is so because the gods love it ; in other words, that the gods loving must be regarded as something coming before the existence of the θεοφιλές, or god-beloved.

(2) That the θεοφιλές cannot with any reason or accuracy be said to be the same thing as the ὅσιον. Euthyphro allows that the gods love a thing because it is holy—Διότι ἄρα ὅσιόν ἐστι φιλεῖται. This, then, is something prior to the gods loving, and if the gods loving is prior to the god-beloved, then, *a fortiori*, the ὅσιον is prior to and greater than the θεοφιλές.

CAP. XIII.

ΣΩ. Τὸ δέ γε θεοφιλὲς ὅτι φιλεῖται ὑπὸ θεῶν, αὐτῷ τούτῳ τῷ φιλεῖσθαι θεοφιλὲς εἶναι, ἀλλ᾽ οὐχ ὅτι θεοφιλές, διὰ τοῦτο φιλεῖσθαι.

ΕΥΘ. Ἀληθῆ λέγεις.

ΣΩ. Ἀλλ᾽ εἴ γε ταὐτὸν ἦν, ὦ φίλε Εὐθύφρον, τὸ θεοφιλὲς καὶ τὸ ὅσιον, εἰ μὲν διὰ τὸ ὅσιον εἶναι ἐφιλεῖτο τὸ ὅσιον, καὶ διὰ τὸ θεοφιλὲς εἶναι ἐφιλεῖτο ἂν τὸ θεοφιλές· εἰ δὲ διὰ τὸ φιλεῖσθαι ὑπὸ 11 θεῶν τὸ θεοφιλὲς θεοφιλὲς ἦν, καὶ τὸ ὅσιον ἂν διὰ τὸ φιλεῖσθαι ὅσιον ἦν. νῦν δὲ ὁρᾷς, ὅτι ἐναντίως ἔχετον, ὡς παντάπασιν ἑτέρω ὄντε ἀλλήλων. τὸ μὲν γάρ, ὅτι φιλεῖται, ἐστὶν οἷον φιλεῖσθαι· τὸ δ᾽ ὅτι ἐστὶν οἷον φιλεῖσθαι, διὰ τοῦτο φιλεῖται. καὶ κινδυνεύεις, ὦ Εὐθύφρον, ἐρωτώμενος τὸ ὅσιον, ὅ τι

Ἀλλ᾽ εἴ γε ταὐτὸν ἦν. Again, premising these three steps— (1) The holy is loved by the gods because it is holy; (2) The gods love certain things; (3) The god-beloved is the result of the gods loving—we can argue thus: If the holy and the god-beloved were the same, from (3), then the holy would be the result of the gods loving; but from (1) the holy is the cause of the gods loving, which is absurd. Next: If the holy and the god-beloved were the same, from (1), the god-beloved would be loved by the gods, because it is god-beloved, i.e. it would be the cause of the gods loving; but from (3) it is the result of the gods loving, which is absurd.

οἷον φιλεῖσθαι, i.e. ὅσιον. "Propter suam ipsius naturam."— Stallb.

ὅτι φιλεῖται, i.e. θεοφιλες: i.e. we place it under the holy things, because we recognise in it the characteristics of the ὅσιον.

τὸ μὲν γάρ... A restatement of the position. The one, viz., the god-beloved, being loved, or because it is loved, is lovable, or "of a kind to be loved" (Jowett), while the other is loved because it is of a kind to be loved. In the latter case the lovable qualities are evident, in the former they need to be drawn out.

καὶ κινδυνεύεις... "So it appears, Euthyphro, that you will not make known to me the true essence of the holy, but only tell me one of its particular cases or manifestations," viz., that all the gods love it. V. S. note on 7, εἶδος. Εἶδος and οὐσία are different names for the same thing, viewed in different lights: εἶδος, the true form or model, exemplar; οὐσία, the really existing, opposed to πάθος, what is experienced (πάσχεται) by men.

E

ποτ᾽ ἔστι, τὴν μὲν οὐσίαν μοι αὐτοῦ οὐ βούλεσθαι
δηλῶσαι, πάθος δέ τι περὶ αὐτοῦ λέγειν, ὅ τι πέ-
B πονθε τοῦτο τὸ ὅσιον, φιλεῖσθαι ὑπὸ πάντων θεῶν·
ὅ τι δὲ ὄν, οὔπω εἶπες. εἰ οὖν σοι φίλον, μή με
ἀποκρύψῃ, ἀλλὰ πάλιν εἰπὲ ἐξ ἀρχῆς, τί ποτε ὂν τὸ
ὅσιον εἴτε φιλεῖται ὑπὸ θεῶν, εἴτε ὁτιδὴ πάσχει. οὐ
γὰρ περὶ τούτου διοισόμεθα· ἀλλ᾽ εἰπὲ προθύμως,
τί ἐστι τό τε ὅσιον καὶ τὸ ἀνόσιον·
ΕΥΘ. Ἀλλ᾽, ὦ Σώκρατες, οὐκ ἔχω ἔγωγε ὅπως
σοι εἴπω ὃ νοῶ. περιέρχεται γάρ πως ἀεὶ ἡμῖν ὃ ἂν
. προθώμεθα, καὶ οὐκ ἐθέλει μένειν ὅπου ἂν᾽ ἱδρυσω-
μεθα αὐτό.
ΣΩ. Τοῦ ἡμετέρου προγόνου, ὦ Εὐθύφρον, ἔοικεν
C εἶναι Δαιδάλου τὰ ὑπὸ σοῦ λεγόμενα. καὶ εἰ μὲν
αὐτὰ ἐγὼ ἔλεγον καὶ ἐτιθέμην, ἴσως ἄν με ἐπέ-
σκωπτες, ὡς ἄρα καὶ ἐμοὶ κατὰ τὴν ἐκείνου ξυγγέ-
νειαν τὰ ἐν τοῖς λόγοις ἔργα ἀποδιδράσκει καὶ οὐκ
ἐθέλει μένειν ὅπου ἄν τις αὐτὰ θῇ· νῦν δέ — σοὶ γὰρ
αἱ ὑποθέσεις εἰσιν—ἄλλου δὴ τινος δεῖ σκώμματος.
οὐ γὰρ ἐθέλουσί σοι μένειν, ὡς καὶ αὐτῷ σοι δοκεῖ. .
ΕΥΘ. Ἐμοὶ δὲ δοκεῖ σχεδὸν τι τοῦ αὐτοῦ σκώμματος, ὦ Σώκρατες, δεῖσθαι τὰ λεγόμενα· τὸ γαρ

ὅ τι πέπονθε τὸ ὅσ... "a particular phase which the holy
undergoes," "one aspect of the
holy." V.S. note on 9, οὐκοῦν,
&c.
B. εἴπω ὃ νοῶ, "express my
thoughts."
περιέρχεται. Sc. to the same
point.
'εἰ μὲν ... νῦν δε, infra.
ἄρα, "as you say."
τοῦ ἡμετέρου προγ. Cf. Alcib.
Maj. 121, A., Socr. καὶ γὰο τὸ
ἡμέτερον, ὦ γενναῖε Ἀλκιβιάδη,
εἰς Δαίδαλον ... (ἀναφέρεται).

C. ἀποδιδράσκει. These were
certain statues or figures en-
dowed with locomotive power.
σοι, with reference to Euthyphro's words, περιέρχεται ...
ἡμῖν ... For σοι V.S. note on
5, διδασκάλῳ.
οὐ ... ἐθέλουσι μένειν, "show
an inclination to be on the
move." Jowett.
τὸ γάρ, &c. "For it is not I
who worked in this locomotion,
this inability to stay in one
place ..."

ΕΥΘΥΦΡΩΝ. 51

περιιέναι αὐτοῖς τοῦτο καὶ μὴ μένειν ἐν τῷ αὐτῷ οὐκ
ἐγώ εἰμι ὁ ἐντιθείς, ἀλλὰ σύ μοι δοκεῖς ὁ Δαίδαλος· D
ἐπεὶ ἐμοῦ γε ἕνεκα ἔμενεν ἂν ταῦτα οὕτως.

ΣΩ. Κινδυνεύω ἄρα, ὦ ἑταῖρε, ἐκείνου τοῦ
ἀνδρὸς δεινότερος γεγονέναι τὴν τέχνην τοσούτῳ, ὅσῳ
ὁ μὲν τὰ αὑτοῦ μόνα ἐποίει οὐ μένοντα, ἐγὼ δὲ
πρὸς τοῖς ἐμαυτοῦ, ὡς ἔοικε, καὶ τὰ ἀλλότρια. καὶ
δῆτα τοῦτό μοι τῆς τέχνης ἐστὶ κομψότατον, ὅτι
ἄκων εἰμὶ σοφός. ἐβουλόμην γὰρ ἄν μοι τοὺς λό-
γους μένειν, καὶ ἀκινήτως ἱδρῦσθαι μᾶλλον ἢ πρὸς Ε
τῇ Δαιδάλου σοφίᾳ τὰ Ταντάλου χρήματα γενέσθαι.
καὶ τούτων μὲν ἅδην. ἐπειδὴ δέ μοι δοκεῖς σὺ τρυφᾶν, αὐτός σοι ξυμπροθυμήσομαι δεῖξαι, ὅπως ἄν
με διδάξαις περὶ τοῦ ὁσίου· καὶ μὴ προαποκάμῃς.

D. ἐμοῦ γε ἕνεκα, "as far as
I am concerned." Cf. Eng.
"for me ;" e.g., "You may go
for me" = "I will not stop
you." So Her. 1, 42, τοῦ φυλάσ-
σοντος εἵνεκεν.
δεινότερος τὴν τέχν. Cf. τὸν
δῆμον Πιτθεύς ; ch. 1 and
note.
τῆς τέχνης, partitive genitive, "amongst the characteristics of my art this one is the
finest."
μᾶλλον ἤ, &c., "rather than
to possess the wealth of Tantalus
besides the cunning of Daedalus."
E. ἅδην, sc. ἔχομεν. "A
truce to this."
τρυφᾶν, "mollem et delicatum
te praebere," Stallb. This verb
expresses the feeling of fas-
tidiousness and effeminacy con-
sequent upon indulgence or deli-
cate living, all which is here
transferred to the intellectual
sphere.
αὐτός σοι, &c. "I will take

pains to help you towards pointing out to me . . ." As it were
infuse the healthy desire of im-
parting real knowledge into one
who already has the power, but
lacks the inclination. By such
an artful manifestation of words
does Socrates try to excite Euthyphro to say all he can for the
question, drawing him on by this
skilful flattery to help the poor
stumbler, as he represents himself, along the road of knowledge.
This little diversion concerning Daedalus, with the remarks
preceding and following, is
thrown in, in a masterly manner,
to rest the mind of the hearer
between the arguments. Socrates is going to begin another
bout on the original question,
but gives his companion a short
breathing time and a slight re-
freshment (this little Daedalus
episode) before again entering
the dialectical lists.

E 2

ιδὲ γάρ· οὐκ ἀναγκαῖόν σοι δοκεῖ δίκαιον εἶναι πᾶν
τὸ ὅσιον ;

ΕΥΘ. Ἔμοιγε.

ΣΩ. Ἆρ᾽ οὖν καὶ πᾶν τὸ δίκαιον ὅσιον, ἢ τὸ
12 μὲν ὅσιον πᾶν δίκαιον, τὸ δὲ δίκαιον οὐ πᾶν ὅσιον,
ἀλλὰ τὸ μὲν αὐτοῦ ὅσιον, τὸ δέ τι καὶ ἄλλο ;
ΕΥΘ. Οὐχ ἕπομαι, ὦ Σάκρατες, τοῖς λεγομένοις.
ΣΩ. Καὶ μὴν νεώτερός γ᾽ ἐμοῦ εἶ οὐκ ἔλαττον ἢ
ὅσῳ σοφώτερος· ἀλλ᾽, ὃ λέγω, τρυφᾷς ὑπὸ πλούτου
τῆς σοφίας. ἀλλ᾽, ὦ μακάριε, ξύντεινε σαυτόν· καὶ
γὰρ οὐδὲ χαλεπὸν κατανοῆσαι ὃ λέγω. λέγω γὰρ δὴ
τὸ ἐναντίον ἢ ὁ ποιητὴς ἐποίησεν ὁ ποιήσας

Ζῆνα δὲ τόν θ᾽ ἔρξαντα, καὶ ὃς τάδε πάντ᾽
ἐφύτευσεν,
Οὐκ ἐθέλεις εἰπεῖν· ἵνα γὰρ δέος, ἔνθα καὶ
αἰδώς.

ἐγὼ οὖν τούτῳ διαφέρομαι τῷ ποιητῇ. ε πω σοι ὅπῃ;

ΕΥΘ. Πάνυ γε.

ΣΩ. Οὐ δοκεῖ μοι εἶναι, ἵνα δέος, ἔνθα καὶ αἰδώς.
πολλοὶ γάρ μοι δοκοῦσι, καὶ νόσους καὶ πενίας καὶ

οὐκ ἀναγκαῖον . . . Socrates
is going to extract from Euthyphro the admission that although
all things holy are just, it is not
true that all just things are holy.
This may be thus geometrically
represented—
A, things just ; B, things
holy.

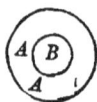

where we see that though no
things holy are not also just,
there are yet some just things
(A) which are not holy (B).

Hence holiness is a part or
species of what justice is the
whole or genus.
τὸ δέ τι. The indefinite pronoun is added because it is not
known *what* part of justice is
covered by holiness, and what
by other virtues. So Lucian,
D. Mort. 16, 5, εἰ γὰρ ὁ μέν τις
ἐν οὐρανῷ, ὁδὲ παρ᾽ ἡμῖν, σὺ τὸ
εἴδωλον, τὸ δὲ σῶμα ἐν Οἴτῃ
κόνις ἤδη γεγένηται, where ὁ
μέν τις is the (indefinable) divine part of Heracles that has
left the earth.
ξύντεινε σ. "brace yourself."
ποιητής. Stasinus, who wrote
the Cypria.

ἄλλα πολλὰ τοιαῦτα δεδιότες, δεδιέναι μέν, αἰδεῖσθαι
δὲ μηδὲν ταῦτα; ἃ δεδίασιν. οὐ καὶ σοὶ δοκεῖ;
ΕΥΘ. Πάνυ γε.
ΣΩ. Ἀλλ᾽ ἵνα γε αἰδώς, ἔνθα καὶ δέος εἶναι·
ἐπεὶ ἔστιν ὅστις αἰδούμενός τι πρᾶγμα καὶ αἰσχυ-
νόμενος οὐ πεφόβηταί τε καὶ δέδοικεν ἅμα δόξα·
πονηρίας;
ΕΥΘ. Δέδοικε μὲν οὖν.
ΣΩ. Οὐκ ἄρ᾽ ὀρθῶς ἔχει λέγειν· ἵνα γὰρ δέος,
ἔνθα καὶ αἰδώς, ἀλλ᾽ ἵνα μὲν αἰδώς, ἔνθα καὶ δέος·
οὐ μέντοι ἵνα γε δέος, πανταχοῦ αἰδώς, ἐπὶ πλέον
γάρ, οἶμαι, δέος αἰδοῦς· μόριον γὰρ αἰδὼς δέους,
ὥσπερ ἀριθμοῦ περιττόν, ὥστε οὐχ ἵνα περ ἀριθμός,
ἔνθα καὶ περιττόν, ἵνα δὲ περιττόν, ἔνθα καὶ ἀριθμός.
ἔπει γάρ που νῦν γε;
ΕΥΘ. Πάνυ γε.
ΣΩ. Τὸ τοιοῦτον τοίνυν καὶ ἐκεῖ λέγων ἠρώτων, ἆρα ἵνα δίκαιον, ἔνθα καὶ ὅσιον, ἢ ἵνα μὲν ὅσιον,
ἔνθα καὶ δίκαιον, ἵνα δὲ δίκαιον, οὐ πανταχοῦ ὅσιον· D

ἀλλ᾽ ἵνα μὲν αἰδώς... This
will be expressed as above, C C
being fear, D being reverence.

All reverence implies fear, but
not all fear reverence. And
there the poet is wrong, for he
makes the two coextensive.
οὐ μέντοι ἵνα γε δέος... γε
qualifies the whole sentence,
being placed as soon as possible
after the beginning of the wrong
statement, to which it calls attention, or which it stigmatises.
ἐπὶ πλέον, &c. "Fear is a
term of wider extension than

reverence, which is a part of
fear."
ὥστε οὐχ, &c. "In the same
way all number is not odd, but
all odd implies number." All
this is to show that, though all
things holy are just, all just
things are not holy—that justice
is the larger head under which
we can range holiness. Definition, logicians tell us, is per
genus et differentiam, i.e. by
giving the genus or family, and
the distinctive marks of the
particular member of the family
we have in view. Justice is the
genus: it remains then to find
the differentia, or distinguishing
marks of this particular phase
of justice called holiness.

μόριον γὰρ τοῦ δικαίου τὸ ὅσιον, οὕτω φῶμεν ἢ ἄλλως
σοι δοκεῖ;

ΕΥΘ. Οὐκ, ἀλλ᾽ οὕτω. φαίνει γάρ μοι ὀρθῶς
λέγειν.

CAP. XIV.

ΣΩ. Ὅρα δὴ τὸ μετὰ τοῦτο. εἰ γὰρ μέρος τὸ ὅσιον
τοῦ δικαίου, δεῖ δὴ ἡμᾶς, ὡς ἔοικεν, ἐξευρεῖν τὸ ποῖον
μέρος ἂν εἴη τοῦ δικαίου τὸ ὅσιον. εἰ μὲν οὖν σύ με
ἠρώτας τι τῶν νῦν δή, οἷον ποῖον μέρος ἐστὶν ἀριθμοῦ
τὸ ἄρτιον καὶ τίς ὢν τυγχάνει οὗτος ὁ ἀριθμός, εἶπον
ἄν, ὅτι ὃς ἂν μὴ σκαληνος ᾖ, ἀλλ᾽ ἰσοσκελής· ἢ οὐ
δοκεῖ σοι;

ΕΥΘ. Ἔμοιγε.

E ΣΩ. Πειρῶ δὴ καὶ σὺ ἐμὲ οὕτω διδάξαι, τὸ ποῖον
μέρος τοῦ δικαίου ὅσιόν ἐστιν, ἵνα καὶ Μελήτῳ
λέγωμεν μηκέθ᾽ ἡμᾶς ἀδικεῖν μηδ᾽ ἀσεβείας γράφεσθαι, ὡς ἱκανῶς ἤδη παρὰ σοῦ μεμαθηκότας τά τε
εὐσεβῆ καὶ ὅσια καὶ τὰ μή.

ΕΥΘ. Τοῦτο τοίνυν ἔμοιγε δοκεῖ, ὦ Σώκρατες,
τὸ μέρος τοῦ δικαίου εἶναι εὐσεβές τε καὶ ὅσιον, τὸ
περὶ τὴν τῶν θεῶν θεραπείαν· τὸ δὲ περὶ τὴν τῶν
ἀνθρώπων τὸ λοιπὸν εἶναι τοῦ δικαίου μέρος.

D. τὸ ἄρτιον, even, conn. w.
ἄρω, ἄρτι, "fitting exactly;"
explained by ἰσοσκελής, equal-
limbed, opposed to σκαληνός,
halting, or with unequal limbs.
These terms are transferred here
from geometry to arithmetic.
E. τοῦτο τοίνυν. Socrates at
last succeeds in getting a further

definition out of Euthyphro,
which he at once proceeds to
test. Euthyphro divides justice
into two parts, perhaps with the
odd and even division of numbers running in his head, into
justice with respect to heaven,
and with respect to men. The
former, he says, is holiness.

CAP. XV.

ΣΩ. Καὶ καλῶς γέ μοι, ὦ Εὐθύφρον, φαίνει λέγειν· ἀλλὰ σμικροῦ τινὸς ἔτι ἐνδεής εἰμι. τὴν γὰρ θερα- 13 πείαν οὔπω ξυνίημι ἥντινα ὀνομάζεις. οὐ γάρ που λέγεις γε, οἷαί περ καὶ αἱ περὶ τὰ ἄλλα θεραπεῖαί εἰσι, τοιαύτην καὶ περὶ θεούς. λέγομεν γάρ που — οἷον φαμέν, ἵππους οὐ πᾶς ἐπίσταται θεραπεύειν, ἀλλ' ὁ ἱππικός· ἢ γάρ;

ΕΥΘ. Πάνυ γε.

ΣΩ. Ἡ γάρ που ἱππικὴ ἵππων θεραπεία.

ΕΥΘ. Ναί.

ΣΩ. Οὐδέ γε κύνας πᾶς ἐπίσταται θεραπεύειν, ἀλλ' ὁ κυνηγετικός.

ΕΥΘ. Οὕτως.

ΣΩ. Ἡ γάρ που κυνηγετικὴ κυνῶν θεραπεία.

ΕΥΘ. Ναί.　　　　　　　　　　　　　　　　　　B

ΣΩ. Ἡ δὲ βοηλατικὴ βοῶν.

ΕΥΘ. Πανυ γε.

ΣΩ. Ἡ δὲ δὴ ὁσιότης τε καὶ εὐσέβεια θεῶν; ὦ Εὐθύφρον· οὕτω λέγεις;

ΕΥΘ. Ἔγωγε.

ΣΩ. Οὐκοῦν θεραπεία γε πᾶσα ταὐτὸν διαπράττεται, οἷον τοιόνδε· ἐπ' ἀγαθῷ τινί ἐστι, καὶ ὠφελείᾳ

ἀλλὰ σμικροῦ. Socrates will not start on the discussion of this definition without having it clearly understood what the words mean.
λέγομεν γάρ που ... Socrates was going to say, "We understand, do we not, that every θεραπεία has its particular art, and cannot be undertaken ex- cept by him who is acquainted with that art." But he breaks off with an example, οἷόν φαμεν, and proceeds to establish the principle in his usual way by aggregating instances.—Stallb.

B. οἷον τοιόνδε, sc. λέγω, as is shown by Rep. 331 C, οἷον τοιόνδε λέγω, πᾶς ἄν που εἴποι ...

56 ΠΛΑΤΩΝΟΣ

τοῦ θεραπευομένου, ὥσπερ ὁρᾷς δή, ὅτι οἱ ἵπποι ὑπο
τῆς ἱππικῆς θεραπευόμενοι ὠφελοῦνται καὶ βελτίους
γίγνονται· ἢ οὐ δοκοῦσί σοι ;

ΕΥΘ. Ἔμοιγε.

C ΣΩ. Καὶ οἱ κύνες γέ που ὑπὸ τῆς κυνηγετικῆς
καὶ οἱ βόες ὑπὸ τῆς βοηλατικῆς, καὶ τἆλλα πάντα
ὡσαύτως· ἢ ἐπὶ βλάβῃ οἴει τοῦ θεραπευομένου τὴν
θεραπείαν εἶναι ;

ΕΥΘ. Μὰ Δι' οὐκ ἔγωγε.

ΣΩ. Ἀλλ' ἐπ' ὠφελείᾳ ;

ΕΥΘ. Πῶς δ' οὔ ;

ΣΩ. Ἦ οὖν καὶ ἡ ὁσιότης θεραπεία οὖσα θεῶν
ὠφέλειά τέ ἐστι θεῶν καὶ βελτίους τοὺς θεοὺς ποιεῖ ;
καὶ σὺ τοῦτο ξυγχωρήσαις ἄν, ὡς ἐπειδάν τι ὅσιον
ποιῇς, βελτίω τινὰ τῶν θεῶν ἀπεργάζει ;

ΕΥΘ. Μὰ Δι οὐκ ἔγωγε.

ΣΩ. Οὐδέ γὰρ ἐγώ, ὦ Εὐθύφρον, οἶμαί σε τοῦτο
λέγειν· πολλοῦ καὶ δέω· ἀλλὰ τούτου δὴ ἕνεκα καὶ
ἀνηρόμην, τίνα ποτὲ λέγοις τὴν θεραπείαν τῶν θεῶν,
D οὐχ ἡγούμενός σε τοιαύτην λέγειν.

ΕΥΘ. Καὶ ὀρθῶς γε, ὦ Σώκρατες· οὐ γὰρ τοιαύτην λέγω.

ΣΩ. Εἶεν· ἀλλὰ τίς δὴ θεῶν θεραπεία εἴη ἂν ἡ
ὁσιότης ;

οἱ ἵπποι. These examples
from common life are very frequently used by Socrates to
establish analogies. Cf. Rep.
335, βλαπτόμενοι δ' ἵπποι βελτίους ἢ χείρους γίγνονται; χείρους.
ἆρα εἰς τὴν τῶν κυνῶν ἀρετὴν ἤ εἰς
τὴν ἵππων; κ.τ.λ.
C. σύ. Perhaps this pronoun
has a distinctive force : "You
the theologian (who can hardly
think so)."

πολλοῦ καὶ δεω. V. S. note
on πολλοῦ, ch. iv.
τούτου δὴ ἕνεκα καὶ ἀνηρόμην
.. οὐχ ἡγούμενος .. "I asked you
for this reason, viz., that I wanted
your repudiation of such an idea."
οὐχ belongs to λέγειν, and ἡγούμενος means more than "think-
ing,"—"Because I expected."
D. τίς δὴ θ., "quod tandem
deorum officium?" acc. of cog-
nate notion.

ΕΥΘ. Ἥνπερ, ὦ Σώκρατες, οἱ δοῦλοι τοὺς δεσπότας θεραπεύουσιν.

ΣΩ. Μανθάνω· ὑπηρετική τις ἄν, ὡς ἔοικεν, εἴη θεοῖς.

ΕΥΘ. Πάνυ μὲν οὖν.

CAP. XVI.

ΣΩ. Ἔχοις ἂν οὖν εἰπεῖν, ἡ ἰατροῖς ὑπηρετικὴ εἰς τίνος ἔργου ἀπεργασίαν τυγχάνει οὖσα ὑπηρετική; οὐκ εἰς ὑγιείας οἴει ;

ἥνπερ ... θερ. Cf. Rep. 5, 456, D, ἀρετὴν ἀντὶ ἱματίων ἀμφιέσονται. Matthiae explains such verbs as governing an accusative on account of the active sense implied in them.

ἡ ἰατροῖς ὑπηρετική. The art, subservient or auxiliary to healing others, which physicians use. Distinguish this carefully from ἡ θεοῖς ὑπηρετική lower down, which means "the art which others use serviceable to the gods for their own benefit."

There is a transition from one sense of θεραπεία and ὑπ ετική to another in this passage. The θεραπεία of dogs, horses, &c., is directed towards their physical improvement. θεραπεία therefore means "care for," without any notion of subservience, but simply the care that every good master or workman gives to the instruments he uses for making a livelihood. But when we come to the answer, ἥνπερ οἱ δοῦλο· τοὺς δεσπότας θεραπεύουσιν, the metaphor changes. It is no longer the mechanic or the herdsman working independently, and giving proper attention to his tools and his beasts, but a servant attending to the different wants and *arbitrary* demands of his master. Notice therefore the distinction drawn above. The θεραπεία ἰατροῖς ὑπηρετική is the course of study and knowledge of detail necessary or ancillary to a physician's right employment of his art ; the result of it is ὑγίεια, health, to the objects of its attention : whilst the θεραπεία θεοῖς ὑπηρετ. is the unreasoning, implicit attention that must be given from an inferior towards a superior in whose service he finds himself. The first θεραπεία is objective, directed towards the accomplishment of an external effect; the second is the discharge of a duty. Plato, however, by preserving the same phraseology with really different meanings, drives Euthyphro to seek for some external good effected by our attention to divine worship and other religious duties, for the benefit of heaven ; instead of perceiving that the consciousness of rectitude must be the chief result of attention to pious duties.

ΕΥΘ. Ἔγωγε.

ΣΩ. Τί δέ; ἡ ναυπηγοῖς ὑπηρετικὴ εἰς τίνος ἔργου ἀπεργασίαν ὑπηρετική ἐστιν;

Ε ΕΥΘ. Δῆλον ὅτι, ὦ Σώκρατες, εἰς πλοίου.

ΣΩ. Καὶ ἡ οἰκοδομοις γέ που εἰς οἰκίας;

ΕΥΘ. Ναί.

ΣΩ. Εἰπὲ δὴ, ὦ ἄριστε· ἡ δὲ θεοῖς ὑπηρετικὴ εἰς τινος ἔργου ἀπεργασίαν ὑπηρετικὴ ἂν εἴη; δῆλον γάρ, ὅτι σὺ οἶσθα ἐπειδήπερ τά γε θεῖα κάλλιστα φῂς εἰδέναι ἀνθρώπων.

ΕΥΘ. Καὶ ἀληθῆ γε λέγω, ὦ Σώκρατες.

ΣΩ. Εἰπὲ δὴ πρὸς Διός, τί ποτ᾽ ἐστὶν ἐκεῖνο τὸ πάγκαλον ἔργον, ὃ οἱ θεοὶ ἀπεργαζονται ἡμῖν ὑπηρέταις χρώμενοι;

ΕΥΘ. Πολλὰ καὶ καλά, ὦ Σώκρατες.

14 ΣΩ. Καὶ γὰρ οἱ στρατηγοί, ὦ φίλε· ἀλλ᾽ ὅμως τὸ κεφάλαιον αὐτῶν ῥᾳδίως ἂν εἴποις, ὅτι νίκην ἐν τῷ πολεμῳ ἀπεργάζονται· ἢ οὔ;

ΕΥΘ. Πῶς δ᾽ οὔ;

ΣΩ. Πολλὰ δέ γ᾽ οἶμαι καὶ καλὰ καὶ οἱ γεωργοί. ἀλλ ὅμως τὸ κεφάλαιον αὐτῶν ἐστι τῆς ἀπεργασίας ἡ ἐκ τῆς γῆς τροφή.

ΕΥΘ. Πάνυ γε.

ΣΩ. Τί δὲ δή; τῶν πολλῶν καὶ καλῶν, ἃ οἱ θεοὶ ἀπεργάζονται, τι τὸ κεφάλαιόν ἐστι τῆς ἀπεργασίας;

Β ΕΥΘ. Καὶ ὀλίγον τοι πρότερον εἶπον, ὦ Σώκρατες, ὅτι πλείονος ἔργου ἐστὶν ἀκριβῶς ταῦτα

ἡμῖν ὑπηρεταις χρώμενοι, V. S. ch. 7, E, χρώμενος αὐτῇ παραδείγματι, and note.
τὸ κεφάλαιον. Understand τῆς ἀπεργασίας before αὐτῶν from the next remark of Socrates.

πλείονος ἔργου. This gen. is explained as follows by Matthiae: "The genitive denotes the person or thing in which anything is found, whether as a property or a quality," &c., &c.

πάντα ὡς ἔχει μαθεῖν· τόδε μέντοι σοι ἁπλῶς λέγω,
ὅτι ἐὰν μὲν κεχαρισμένα τις ἐπίστηται τοῖς θεοῖς
λέγειν τε καὶ πράττειν εὐχόμενός τε καὶ θύων, ταῦτ'
ἔστι τὰ ὅσια, καὶ σώζει τὰ τοιαῦτα τούς τε ἰδίους
οἴκους καὶ τὰ κοινὰ τῶν πόλεων· τὰ δ' ἐναντία τῶν
κεχαρισμένων ἀσεβῆ, ἃ δὴ καὶ ἀνατρέπει ἅπαντα καὶ
ἀπόλλυσιν.

CAP. XVII.

ΣΩ. Ἦ πολύ μοι διὰ βραχυτέρων, ὦ Εὐθύφρον,
εἰ ἐβούλου, εἶπες ἂν τὸ κεφάλαιον ὧν ἠρώτων. ἀλλὰ
γὰρ οὐ πρόθυμός με εἶ διδάξαι· δῆλος εἶ, καὶ γὰρ νῦν
ἐπειδὴ ἐπ' αὐτῷ ἦσθα, ἀπετράπου· ὃ εἰ ἀπεκρίνω, C
ἱκανῶς ἂν ἤδη παρὰ σοῦ τὴν ὁσιότητα ἐμεμαθήκη.
νῦν δέ—ἀνάγκη γὰρ τὸν ἐρωτῶντα τῷ ἐρωτωμένῳ
ἀκολουθεῖν, ὅπῃ ἂν ἐκεῖνος ὑπάγῃ· τί δὴ αὖ λέγεις
τὸ ὅσιον εἶναι καὶ τὴν ὁσιότητα; οὐχὶ ἐπιστήμην
τινὰ τοῦ θύειν τε καὶ εὔχεσθαι;
ΕΥΘ. Ἔγωγε.
ΣΩ. Οὐκοῦν τὸ θύειν δωρεῖσθαί ἐστι τοῖς θεοῖς,
τὸ δ' εὔχεσθαι αἰτεῖν τοὺς θεούς;
ΕΥΘ. Καὶ μάλα, ὦ Σώκρατες.
ΣΩ. Ἐπιστήμη ἄρα αἰτήσεως καὶ δόσεως θεοῖς D
ἡ ὁσιότης ἂν εἴη, ἐκ τούτου τοῦ λόγου.
ΕΥΘ. Πάνυ καλῶς, ὦ Σώκρατες, ξυνῆκας ὃ εἶπον.
ΣΩ. Ἐπιθυμητὴς γάρ εἰμι, ὦ φίλε, τῆς σῆς σοφίας

Here we may say not a property
or a quality, but a species or
part of a genus or whole, and
refer it to the general head of
the partitive genitive, "is a
matter of further exertion."
B. σώζει, "saves," i.e. from

στασις or dispute, as we see from
the corresponding words, ἀνατρέπει καὶ ἀπόλλ.
πολύ, join to βραχυτέρων.
δῆλος εἶ, plane videris.
C. ἐπ' αὐτῷ ἦσθα. Cf. Rep.
532, τότε δὴ ἐπ' αὐτῷ γίγνεται.

καὶ προσέχω τὸν νοῦν αὐτῇ· ὥστε οὐ χαμαὶ πεσεῖται
ὅ τι ἂν εἴπῃς· ἀλλά μοι λέξον, τίς αὕτη ἡ ὑπηρεσία
ἐστί τοῖς θεοῖς; αἰτεῖν τε φῂς αὐτοὺς καὶ διδόναι
ἐκείνοις;
ΕΥΘ. Ἔγωγε.

CAP. XVIII.

ΣΩ. Ἆρ᾽ οὖν οὐ τὸ ὀρθῶς αἰτεῖν ἂν εἴη, ὧν δεό-
μεθα παρ᾽ ἐκείνων, ταῦτα αὐτοὺς αἰτεῖν;
ΕΥΘ. Ἀλλὰ τί;
ΣΩ. Καὶ αὖ τὸ διδόναι ὀρθῶς, ὧν ἐκεῖνοι τυγχάνουσι δεόμενοι παρ᾽ ἡμῶν ταῦτα ἐκείνοις αὖ ἀντι-
E δωρεῖσθαι; οὐ γάρ που τεχνικόν γ᾽ ἂν εἴη δωροφορεῖν
διδόντα τῳ ταῦτα, ὧν οὐδὲν δεῖται.
ΕΥΘ. Ἀληθῆ λέγεις, ὦ Σώκρατες.
ΣΩ. Ἐμπορικὴ ἄρα τις ἂν εἴη, ὦ Εὐθύφρον,
τέχνη ἡ ὁσιότης θεοῖς καὶ ἀνθρώποις παρ᾽ ἀλλήλων.
ΕΥΘ. Ἐμπορική, εἰ οὕτως ἥδιόν σοι ὀνομάζειν.
ΣΩ. Ἀλλ᾽ οὐδὲν ἥδιον ἔμοιγε, εἰ μὴ τυγχάνει
ἀληθὲς ὄν. φράσον δέ μοι, τίς ἡ ὠφέλεια τοῖς θεοῖς
τυγχάνει οὖσα ἀπὸ τῶν δώρων ὧν παρ᾽ ἡμῶν λαμβά-
15 νουσιν; ἃ μὲν γὰρ διδόασι, παντὶ δῆλον· οὐδὲν γὰρ
ἡμῖν ἐστὶν ἀγαθόν, ὅ τι ἂν μὴ ἐκεῖνοι δῶσιν· ἃ δὲ
παρ᾽ ἡμῶν λαμβάνουσι, τί ὠφελοῦνται; ἢ τοσοῦτον
αὐτῶν πλεονεκτοῦμεν κατὰ τὴν ἐμπορίαν, ὥστε πάντα
τἀγαθὰ παρ᾽ αὐτῶν λαμβάνομεν, ἐκεῖνοι δὲ παρ᾽
ἡμῶν οὐδέν;

D. ἀλλὰ τί. sc. ἄλλο.
E. οὐ γάρ που... Cf. Rep.
374, B, ἡ περὶ τὸν πόλεμον
ἀγωνία οὐ τεχνικὴ δοκεῖ εἶναι;
"Is it not of the nature of an

art?" So here, "It does not
seem to be of the nature of an
art that one should give," &c.
ἃ δέ... Omission of ante-
cedent.

ΕΥΘ. Ἀλλ᾽ οἴει, ὦ Σώκρατες, τοὺς θεοὺς ὠφε-
λεῖσθαι ἀπὸ τούτων, ἃ παρ᾽ ἡμῶν λαμβάνουσιν;

ΣΩ. Ἀλλὰ τί δήποτ᾽ ἂν εἴη ταῦτα, ὦ Εὐθύφρον,
τὰ παρ᾽ ἡμῶν δῶρα τοῖς θεοῖς;

ΕΥΘ. Τί δ᾽ οἴει ἄλλο ἢ τιμή τε καὶ γέρα καὶ
ὅπερ ἐγὼ ἄρτι ἔλεγον, χάρις;

ΣΩ. Κεχαρισμένον ἄρα ἐστίν, ὦ Εὐθύφρον, τὸ B
ὅσιον, ἀλλ᾽ οὐχὶ ὠφέλιμον οὐδὲ φίλον τοῖς θεοῖς;

ΕΥΘ. Οἶμαι ἔγωγε πάντων γε μάλιστα φίλον.

ΣΩ. Τοῦτο ἄρ᾽ ἐστὶν αὖ, ὡς ἔοικε, τὸ ὅσιον, τὸ
τοῖς θεοῖς φίλον.

ΕΥΘ. Μάλιστά γε.

CAP. XIX.

ΣΩ. Θαυμάσει οὖν ταῦτα λέγων, ἐὰν σοι οἱ λόγοι
φαίνωνται μὴ μένοντες, ἀλλὰ βαδίζοντες, καὶ ἐμὲ
αἰτιάσει τὸν Δαίδαλον βαδίζοντας αὐτοὺς ποιεῖν,
αὐτὸς ὢν πολύ γε τεχνικώτερος τοῦ Δαιδάλου καὶ
κύκλῳ περιιόντας ποιῶν; ἢ οὐκ αἰσθάνει, ὅτι ὁ λόγος
ἡμῖν περιελθὼν πάλιν εἰς ταὐτὸν ἥκει; μέμνησαι C
γάρ που, ὅτι ἐν τῷ ἔμπροσθεν τό τε ὅσιον καὶ τὸ
θεοφιλὲς οὐ ταὐτὸν ἡμῖν ἐφάνη, ἀλλ᾽ ἕτερα ἀλλήλων·
ἢ οὐδὲ μέμνησαι;

ΕΥΘ. Ἔγωγε.

ΣΩ. Νῦν οὖν οὐκ ἐννοεῖς, ὅτι τὸ τοῖς θεοῖς
φίλον φὴς ὅσιον εἶναι; τοῦτο δὲ ἄλλο τι ἢ θεοφιλὲς
γίγνεται; ἢ οὔ;

τί δήποτ᾽. "What name shall
we give?" "What are we to
call?"

B. μάλιστα φίλον. Thereby
bringing the question round to
its original starting-point. The
question is put in the negative
form, that this answer of Euthyphro's may be more emphatic
and uncompromising.

C. ἐν τῷ ἔμπροσθεν. Ch. 12
ad fin.

ΕΥΘ. Πάνυ γε.

ΣΩ. Οὐκοῦν ἡ ἄρτι οὐ καλῶς ὡμολογοῦμεν, ἢ εἰ τότε καλῶς, νῦν οὐκ ὀρθῶς τιθέμεθα.

ΕΥΘ. Ἔοικεν.

CAP. XX.

D ΣΩ. Ἐξ ἀρχῆς ἄρα ἡμῖν πάλιν σκεπτέον, τι ἐστι τὸ ὅσιον· ὡς ἐγώ, πρὶν ἂν μάθω, ἑκὼν εἶναι οὐκ ἀποδειλιάσω. ἀλλὰ μή με ἀτιμάσῃς, ἀλλὰ παντὶ τρόπῳ προσέχων τὸν νοῦν ὅ τι μάλιστα νῦν εἰπὲ τὴν ἀλήθειαν. οἶσθα γάρ, εἴπερ τις ἄλλος ἀνθρώπων, καὶ οὐκ ἀφετέος εἶ, ὥσπερ ὁ Πρωτεύς, πρὶν ἂν εἴπῃς. εἰ γὰρ μὴ ᾔδησθα σαφῶς τό τε ὅσιον καὶ τὸ ἀνόσιον, οὐκ ἔστιν ὅπως ἂν ποτε ἐπεχείρησας ὑπὲρ ἀνδρὸς θητὸς ἄνδρα πρεσβύτην πατέρα διωκάθειν φόνου, ἀλλὰ καὶ τοὺς θεοὺς ἂν ἔδεισας παρα-
E κινδυνεύειν, μὴ οὐκ ὀρθῶς αὐτὸ ποιήσοις, καὶ τοὺς ἀνθρώπους ᾐσχύνθης. νῦν δὲ εὖ οἶδ᾽, ὅτι σαφῶς οἴει εἰδέναι τό τε ὅσιον καὶ μή. εἰπὲ οὖν, ὦ βέλτιστε Εὐθύφρον, καὶ μὴ ἀποκρύψῃ ὅ τι αὐτὸ ἡγεῖ.

ΕΥΘ. Εἰσαῦθις τοίνυν, ὦ Σώκρατες. νῦν γὰρ σπεύδω ποι, καί μοι ὥρα ἀπιέναι.

ΣΩ. Οἷα ποιεῖς, ὦ ἑταῖρε· ἀπ᾽ ἐλπίδος με κα-ταβαλὼν μεγάλης ἀπέρχει, ἣν εἶχον, ὡς παρὰ σοῦ

D. ὡς ἐγώ, understand ἴσθι.
" Be sure I will not . . ."
ἑκὼν εἶναι. Jelf's explanation of this phrase seems scarcely likely : he compares θείειν ἄριστος, and makes εἶναι = οὐσίαν, " Willing in real earnest." To

this example Matthiae adds θέμις εἶναι, σύμπαν εἶναι, τήμερον εἶναι.
εἴπερ τις ἄλλος. Socrates' last attempt on the self-complacency of Euthyphro.
ἔδεισας. This word must be taken both with θεούς and παρακ.

μαθὼν τά τε ὅσια καὶ μὴ καὶ τῆς πρὸς Μέλητον
γραφῆς ἀπαλλάξυμαι, ἐνδειξάμενος ἐκείνῳ ὅτι σοφὸς 16
ἤδη παρ' Εὐθύφρονος τὰ θεῖα γέγονα καὶ ὅτι οὐ-
κέτι ὑπ' ἀγνοίας αὐτοσχεδιάζω οὐδὲ καινοτομῶ
περὶ αὐτά, καὶ δὴ καὶ τὸν ἄλλον βίον ὅ τι ἄμεινον
βιωσοίμην.

E. ἀπαλλάξομαι . . . βιωσοίμην. Schleiermacher and Engle-
hardt make these two verbs
depend on εἶχον, as the nearer
and remoter result, respectively,
of the indicative proposition " I
hoped." For this compare the
well-known passage in Thucydides—παρανίσχον . . . φρυκτοὺς
ὅπως ἀσαφῆ τὰ σημεῖα ᾖ, καὶ μὴ
βοηθοῖεν. Stallb. condemns this
on the ground that we shall have
a " constructio difficilis et contorta ; " and that Socrates will
be undertaking to live a better
life than Euthyphro (ἄμεινον
βιωσοίμην), whom he has already
confessed to be "innocens et

integer" (3 A). But ἄμεινον may
very well refer simply to an
improvement in Socrates' own
moral condition. And as for
the construction, it must be
noticed that Stallbaum's is open
to precisely the same objection
which he brings against Schleiermacher's and Engelhardt's, for
we have the unusual sequence
no less, viz. ἐνδειξάμενος . . . ὅτι
γέγονα . . . καὶ βιωσοίμην, no
less " difficilis et contorta."
And this construction will have
to be explained in just the
same way as that of Schleiermacher, and with greater difficulty.

.

EXCURSUS.

ON THE CHARACTER OF EUTHYPHRO.

In Greek history there is a certain character of whom the hero of this Dialogue strongly reminds us, and this character is Nicias. Nicias was a man of exemplary piety, and so is Euthyphro. Nicias' actions were almost invariably governed by principle, and the same can be said of Euthyphro. Both were highly superstitious—δεισιδαίμονες—in an age when superstition meant rather extreme reverence for everything divine, and was viewed more as a commendable than as a vulgar weakness. And both are presented to our view in situations where their bigotry shows as melancholy as it is preposterous; thus the one refuses to take advantage of the only hope of escape left to a large army reduced to the last extremity of famine, disease, and desperation, because the moon is eclipsed and must be propitiated; whilst the other is calmly proceeding to the arraignment of his own father on a charge of murdering a wretched serf. The serf, it should be remarked, is a murderer himself, and died of exposure (or wilful neglect, as his son Euthyphro no doubt intended to depose before the dicasts).

With this singular plea does Euthyphro first come

F

before our notice. Let it not be supposed that the idea of such an action at law is absurd, and that we have here only a caricature. Turning to the picture of Athenian neglect or positive ill-treatment of the old, we read in the *Acharnians* of Aristophanes as follows :—

οἱ γέροντες οἱ παλαιοὶ μεμφίμεσθα τῇ πόλει.
οὐ γὰρ ἀξίως ἐκείνων ὧν ἐναυμαχήσαμεν
γηροβοσκούμεσθ᾽ ὑφ᾽ ὑμῶν, ἀλλὰ δεινὰ πάσχομεν.
οἵτινες γέροντας ἄνδρας ἐμβαλόντες ἐς γραφὰς
ὑπὸ νεανίσκων ἐᾶτε καταγελᾶσθαι ῥητόρων.—676, &c.

(the exact case in point).

And again, in *Wasps*, 605, &c., if the father comes home with his fee, well and good, all the family are glad to see him ; and if he comes without it—

κεἰ μή με δεήσει
ἐς σὲ βλέψαι καὶ τὸν ταμίαν, ὁπότ᾽ ἄριστον παραθήσει
καταρασάμενος καὶ τονθορύσας. ἄλλην μή μοι ταχὺ μάξῃ.

i.e. "lest he mix me (ἄλλην μᾶζαν) a deadly cake."— Mahaffy. And yet once more, a sad but decisive instance, from the *Clouds*, 844 seqq. :—

οἴμο., τί δράσω παραφρονοῦντος τοῦ πατρός ;
πότερα παρανοίας αὐτὸν εἰσαγαγὼν ἕλω ;
ἢ τοῖς σοροπηγοῖς τὴν μανίαν αὐτοῦ φράσω ;

" My father is mad—let me see. Shall I bring him into court, or get a coffin ready for him ? "

With these instances before us, we can see that this situation, as described by Euthyphro, need not be much exaggerated. Plato has probably given us here a typical and extreme case of unfilial bearing at Athens.

But whilst admitting the case to be an extreme one, we must give Euthyphro his due. Now his self-sufficiency appears by turns absurd, irritating, and impressive. He could no more be persuaded that his course of action admitted of error than he could explain the nature of Right and Wrong to Socrates. Thus, in Ch. IV. E, when relating how this prosecution of his father did not seem quite justifiable to his relatives, he describes them as κακῶς εἰδότες τὸ θεῖον ὡς ἔχει τοῦ ὁσίου τε πέρι καὶ τοῦ ἀνοσίου—" taking a wrong view of divine matters with respect to what is holy and unholy." This is the self-complacency of a man who thoroughly believes in his creed. And so again, in the same chapter, when examined by Socrates as to his confidence in his proceedings, he replies: οὐδὲν γὰρ ἄν μου ὄφελος εἴη, ὦ Σώκρατες, οὐδέ τῳ ἂν διαφέροι Εὐθύφρων τῶν πολλῶν ἀνθρώπων, εἰ μὴ τὰ τοιαῦτα πάντα ἀκριβῶς εἰδείην.

In fact, his knowledge of things divine seems to reach to an extent undreamed of by the ordinary citizen ; thus ὅπερ ἄρτι εἶπον, καὶ ἄλλα σοι ἐγὼ πολλὰ, ἐάνπερ βούλῃ, περὶ τῶν θείων διηγήσομαι, ἃ σὺ ἀκούων εἶ οἶδ᾽ ὅτι ἐκπλαγήσει.

To take another instance at once of his self-sufficiency and his immovable religious convictions, in Ch. IV. B, γελοῖον, ὦ Σώκρατες ὅτι οἴει τι διαφέρειν εἴτε ἀλλότριος εἴτε οἰκεῖος ὁ τεθνεώς. And again of the former quality Ch. V. C, εὕροιμ᾽ ἂν, ὡς οἶμαι, ὅπη σαθρός ἐστι, καὶ πολὺ ἂν ἡμῖν πρότερον περὶ ἐκείνου λόγος γένοιτο ἐν τῷ δικαστηρίῳ, ἢ περὶ ἐμοῦ. From this we see that his self-reliance extended beyond the sphere of religious dogma to that of forensic contention ; for we cannot understand him here as relying merely on his superior knowledge of the subject : the Athenians laugh at that. He himself says (Ch. II. C): "No, he is going to assume the offensive and pick holes in his opponent's case."

But with all this confidence in his argumentative powers we do not find him an apt dialectician. He is unable to see the force of the logical text that, if all A is B it does not follow that all B is A: Ch. III. A., Ἆρ᾽ οὖν καὶ πᾶν τὸ δίκαιον ὅσιον, &c , precc. et. seqq.

He is also sorely bewildered by Socrates' question,
" Is the holy loved by heaven because holy, or is it holy
because loved by heaven ?" And when that question
has been proved the last step has to be explained over
again before he can see the bearing of it, Ch. XII. E.
In Ch. XIII. B. he is fairly reduced to confusion, and
plaintively urges that the argument *will* come round in
a circle, and will not stay where it is put. That he has
a touch of the rhetor in his character we notice from his
paraphrase of Socrates' version of piety in Ch. XVI. A,
where he escapes from the logical difficulty (of telling
what are the ἔργα of God towards which he is assisted
by human attention) under a rather eloquent statement
of what he considers piety to be. He is finally wearied
of the argument, and escapes by means of the plea of
another engagement.

There is a question suggested by the character of
Euthyphro with regard to his own profession. Why
was he not ἐξηγητής, or expounder of religious legislation ? Who so fitted for the task as one ὃς πάντα τὰ
θεῖα ἀκριβῶς εἰδείη ? Who could have expounded the will
of heaven with such incontrovertible emphasis, such
quieting conviction, as Euthyphro ? To be sure he was
not quite proof against a dialectical attack; but then
dialecticians generally managed their own religious
affairs, and would not be likely to trouble the state
servant. He seems, too, to have been a free Athenian,
and presumably of good family. The office of Exegetes·
seems, however, to have been confined to the noble
family of the Eumolpidae. Apart from this restriction,
we can imagine no one better fitted for the office than
Euthyphro, especially in his own eyes. The most
pleasing trait in his character is his unaffected
expression of feeling towards Socrates anent his

prosecution by Meletus, of whom he says, κακουργεῖν τὴν πόλιν ἐπιχειρῶν ἀδικεῖν σε. That he was not a man of unkindly feeling is clear from this passage and the general tone of the Dialogue. This being granted, serves to bring out with greater clearness the extraordinary strength of his creed, requiring as it did the prosecution of his own father for a capital crime, and scattering all such feelings as filial affection to the winds.

Only in Roman history can we find bigotry to parallel Euthyphro's, viz., in the person of Cato the Younger. The two men exhibit the same uncompromising and predetermined attitude towards any attempt to divert them from their convictions. And herein lies the difference between Euthyphro and Nicias, viz., that whilst opposition to the latter sometimes produced irresolution, it only serves to confirm the former in his purpose. And thus on Socrates proving for the third time that Euthyphro is ignorant of the true nature of Right and Wrong, and calling his attention to the wickedness of prosecuting a father without being prepared to show just ground for such a step, Euthyphro calmly takes down Socrates' appeal for instruction as though it were no hint to himself of his ignorance, and replies, Εἰσαῦθις τοίνυν, ὦ Σώκρατες.

THE END.

LONDON :

R. CLAY, SONS, AND TAYLOR,

BREAD STREET HILL, E.C.

LONDON: GEORGE BELL AND SONS.

A CLASSIFIED LIST

OF

EDUCATIONAL WORKS

PUBLISHED BY

GEORGE BELL & SONS.

Full Catalogues will be sent post free on application.

BIBLIOTHECA CLASSICA.

A Series of Greek and Latin Authors, with English Notes, edited by eminent Scholars. 8vo.

Æschylus. By F. A. Paley, M.A. 18s.

Cicero's Orations. By G. Long, M.A. 4 vols. 16s., 14s., 16s., 18s.

Demosthenes. By R. Whiston, M.A. 2 vols. 16s. each.

Euripides. By F. A. Paley, M.A. 3 vols. 16s. each.

Homer. By F. A. Paley, M.A. Vol. I. 12s.; Vol. II. 14s.

Herodotus. By Rev. J. W. Blakesley, B.D. 2 vols. 32s.

Hesiod. By F. A. Paley, M.A. 10s. 6d.

Horace. By Rev. A. J. Macleane, M.A. 18s.

Juvenal and Persius. By Rev. A. J. Macleane, M.A. 12s.

Plato. By W. H. Thompson, D.D. 2 vols. 7s. 6d. each.

Sophocles. Vol. I. By Rev. F. H. Blaydes, M.A. 18s.

—————— Vol. II. Philoctetes. Electra. Ajax and Trachiniæ. By F. A. Paley, M.A. 12s.

Tacitus: The Annals. By the Rev. P. Frost. 15s.

Terence. By E. St. J. Parry, M.A. 18s.

Virgil. By J. Conington, M.A. 3 vols. 14s. each.

An Atlas of Classical Geography; Twenty-four Maps. By W. Hughes and George Long, M.A. New edition, with coloured outlines. Imperial 8vo. 12s. 6d.

Uniform with above.

A Complete Latin Grammar. By J. W. Donaldson, D.D. 3rd Edition. 14s.

GRAMMAR-SCHOOL CLASSICS.

A Series of Greek and Latin Authors, with English Notes. Fcap. 8vo.

Cæsar: De Bello Gallico. By George Long, M.A. 5s. 6d.

—————— Books I.-III. For Junior Classes. By G. Long, M.A. 2s. 6d.

Catullus, Tibullus, and Propertius. Selected Poems. With Life. By Rev. A. H. Wratislaw. 3s. 6d.

Cicero: De Senectute, De Amicitia, and Select Epistles. By
George Long, M.A. 4s. 6d.

Cornelius Nepos. By Rev. J. F. Macmichael. 2s. 6d.

Homer: Iliad. Books I.–XII. By F. A. Paley, M.A. 6s. 6d.

Horace. With Life. By A. J. Macleane, M.A. 6s. 6d. [In
2 parts. 3s. 6d. each.]

Juvenal: Sixteen Satires. By H. Prior, M.A. 4s. 6d.

Martial: Select Epigrams. With Life. By F. A. Paley, M.A. 6s. 6d.

Ovid: the Fasti. By F. A. Paley, M.A. 5s.

Sallust: Catilina and Jugurtha. With Life. By G. Long, M.A. 5s.

Tacitus: Germania and Agricola. By Rev. P. Frost. 3s. 6d.

Virgil: Bucolics, Georgics, and Æneid, Books I.–IV. Abridged
from Professor Conington's Edition. 5s. 6d.—Æneid, Books V.–XII. 5s. 6d.
Also in 9 separate Volumes, 1s. 6d. each.

Xenophon: The Anabasis. With Life. By Rev. J. F. Macmichael. 5s.
Also in 4 separate volumes, 1s. 6d. each.

———— The Cyropædia. By G. M. Gorham, M.A. 6s.

———— Memorabilia. By Percival Frost, M.A. 4s. 6d.

A Grammar-School Atlas of Classical Geography, containing
Ten selected Maps. Imperial 8vo. 5s.

Uniform with the Series.

The New Testament, in Greek. With English Notes, &c. By
Rev. J. F. Macmichael. 7s. 6d.

CAMBRIDGE GREEK AND LATIN TEXTS.

Æschylus. By F. A. Paley, M.A. 3s.

Cæsar: De Bello Gallico. By G. Long, M.A. 2s.

Cicero: De Senectute et de Amicitia, et Epistolæ Selectæ. By
G. Long, M.A. 1s. 6d.

Ciceronis Orationes. Vol. I. (in Verrem.) By G. Long, M.A. 3s. 6d.

Euripides. By F. A. Paley, M.A. 3 vols. 3s. 6d. each.

Herodotus. By J. G. Blakesley, B.D. 2 vols. 7s.

Homeri Ilias. I.–XII. By F. A. Paley, M.A. 2s. 6d.

Horatius. By A. J. Macleane, M.A. 2s. 6d.

Juvenal et Persius. By A. J. Macleane, M.A. 1s. 6d.

Lucretius. By H. A. J. Munro, M.A. 2s. 6d.

Sallusti Crispi Catilina et Jugurtha. By G. Long, M.A. 1s. 6d.

Sophocles. By F. A. Paley, M.A.   [*In the press.*

Terenti Comœdiæ. By W. Wagner, Ph.D. 3s.

Thucydides. By J. G. Donaldson, D.D. 2 vols. 7s.

Virgilius. By J. Conington, M.A. 3s. 6d.

Xenophontis Expeditio Cyri. By J. F. Macmichael, B.A. 2s. 6d.

Novum Testamentum Græcum. By F. H. Scrivener, M.A.
4s. 6d. An edition with wide margin for notes, half bound, 12s.

CAMBRIDGE TEXTS WITH NOTES.
A Selection of the most usually read of the Greek and Latin Authors,
Annotated for Schools. *Fcap. 8vo.* 1s. 6d. *each.,* *with exceptions.*

Euripides. Alcestis.—Medea.—Hippolytus.—Hecuba.—Bacchæ.
Ion. 2s.—Orestes.—Phoenissæ.—Troades. By F. A. Paley, M.A.
Æschylus. Prometheus Vinctus.—Septem contra Thebas.—Agamemnon.—Persæ.—Eumenides. By F. A. Paley, M.A.
Sophocles. Œdipus Tyrannus.—Œdipus Coloneus.—Antigone.
By F. A. Paley, M.A.
Homer. Iliad. Book I. By F. A. Paley, M.A. 1s.
Cicero's De Senectute—De Amicitia and Epistolæ Selectæ. By
G. Long, M.A.
Ovid. Selections. By A. J. Macleane, M.A.
Others in preparation.

PUBLIC SCHOOL SERIES.
A Series of Classical Texts, annotated by well-known Scholars. *Cr. 8vo.*
Aristophanes. The Peace. By F. A. Paley, M.A. 4s. 6d.
———— The Acharnians. By F. A. Paley, M.A. 4s. 6d.
———— The Frogs. By F. A. Paley, M.A. 4s. 6d.
Cicero. The Letters to Atticus. Bk. I. By A. Pretor, M.A. 4s. 6d.
Demosthenes de Falsa Legatione. By R. Shilleto, M.A. 6s.
———— The Law of Leptines. By B. W. Beatson, M.A. 3s. 6d.
Plato. The Apology of Socrates and Crito. By W. Wagner, Ph.D.
6th Edition. 4s. 6d.
———— The Phædo. 6th Edition. By W. Wagner, Ph.D. 5s. 6d.
———— The Protagoras. 3rd Edition. By W. Wayte, M.A. 4s. 6d.
———— The Euthyphro. 2nd edition. By G. H. Wells. 3s.
———— The Euthydemus. By G. H. Wells. 4s.
———— The Republic. By G. H. Wells. [*Preparing.*
Plautus. The Aulularia. By W. Wagner, Ph.D. 2nd edition. 4s. 6d.
———— Trinummus. By W. Wagner, Ph.D. 2nd edition. 4s. 6d.
———— The Menaechmei. By W. Wagner, Ph.D. 4s. 6d.
Sophoclis Trachiniæ. By A. Pretor, M.A. 4s. 6d.
Terence. By W. Wagner, Ph.D. 10s. 6d.
Theocritus. By F. A. Paley, M.A. 4s. 6d.
Others in preparation.

CRITICAL AND ANNOTATED EDITIONS.
Ætna. By H. A. J. Munro, M.A. 3s. 6d.
Aristophanis Comœdiæ. By H. A. Holden, LL.D. 8vo. 2 vols.
23s. 6d. Plays sold separately.
———— Pax. By F. A. Paley, M.A. Fcap. 8vo. 4s. 6d.
Catullus. By H. A. J. Munro, M.A. 7s. 6d.
Corpus Poetarum Catinorum. Edited by Walker. 1 vol. 8vo. 18s.
Horace. Quinti Horatii Flacci Opera. By H. A. J. Munro, M.A.
Large 8vo. 1l. 1s.
Livy. The first five Books. By J. Prendeville. 12mo. roan, 5s.
Or Books I.-III. 3s. 6d. IV. and V. 3s. 6d.

Lucretius. Titi Lucretii Cari de Rerum Natura Libri Sex. With
a Translation and Notes. By H. A. J. Munro, M.A. 2 vols. 8vo. Vol. I.
Text. (New Edition, Preparing.) Vol. II. Translation. (Sold separately.)

Ovid. P. Ovidii Nasonis Heroides XIV. By A. Palmer, M.A. 8vo. 6s.

Propertius. Sex Aurelii Propertii Carmina. By F. A. Paley, M.A.
8vo. Cloth, 9s.

Sex. Propertii Elegiarum. Lib. IV. By A. Palmer. Fcap. 8vo. 5s.

Sophocles. The Ajax. By C. E. Palmer, M.A. 4s. 6d.

Thucydides. The History of the Peloponnesian War. By Richard
Shilleto, M.A. Book I. 8vo. 6s. 6d. Book II. 8vo. 5s. 6d.

LATIN AND GREEK CLASS-BOOKS.

Auxilia Latina. A Series of Progressive Latin Exercises. By
M. J. B. Baddeley, M.A. Fcap. 8vo. Part I. Accidence. 1s. 6d. Part II.
3rd Edition, 2s. Key, 2s. 6d.

Latin Prose Lessons. By Prof. Church, M.A. 6th Edit. Fcap. 8vo.
2s. 6d.

Latin Exercises and Grammar Papers. By T. Collins, M.A. 3rd
Edition. Fcap. 8vo. 2s. 6d.

Unseen Papers in Prose and Verse. With Examination Questions.
By T. Collins, M.A. 2nd edition. Fcap. 8vo. 2s. 6d.

Analytical Latin Exercises. By C. P. Mason, B.A. 3rd Edit. 3s. 6d.

Scala Graeca: a Series of Elementary Greek Exercises. By Rev. J. W.
Davis, M.A., and R. W. Baddeley, M.A. 3rd Edition. Fcap. 8vo. 2s. 6d.

Greek Verse Composition. By G. Preston, M.A. Crown 8vo. 4s. 6d.

BY THE REV. P. FROST, M.A., ST. JOHN'S COLLEGE, CAMBRIDGE.

Eclogae Latinae; or, First Latin Reading-Book, with English Notes
and a Dictionary. New Edition. Fcap. 8vo. 2s. 6d.

Materials for Latin Prose Composition. New Edition. Fcap. 8vo.
2s. 6d. Key, 4s.

A Latin Verse-Book. An Introductory Work on Hexameters and
Pentameters. New Edition. Fcap. 8vo. 3s. Key, 5s.

Analecta Graeca Minora, with Introductory Sentences, English
Notes, and a Dictionary. New Edition. Fcap. 8vo. 3s. 6d.

Materials for Greek Prose Composition. New Edit. Fcap. 8vo.
3s. 6d. Key, 5s.

Florilegium Poeticum. Elegiac Extracts from Ovid and Tibullus.
New Edition. With Notes. Fcap. 8vo. 3s.

BY THE REV. F. E. GRETTON.

A First Cheque-book for Latin Verse-makers. 1s. 6d.

A Latin Version for Masters. 2s. 6d.

Reddenda; or Passages with Parallel Hints for Translation into
Latin Prose and Verse. Crown 8vo. 4s. 6d.

Reddenda Reddita (*see next page*).

BY H. A. HOLDEN, LL.D.

Foliorum Silvula. Part I. Passages for Translation into Latin
Elegiac and Heroic Verse. 9th Edition. Post 8vo. 7s. 6d.

—— Part II. Select Passages for Translation into Latin Lyric
and Comic Iambic Verse. 3rd Edition. Post 8vo. 5s.

—— Part III. Select Passages for Translation into Greek Verse.
3rd Edition. Post 8vo. 8s.

Folia Silvulæ, sive Eclogæ Poetarum Anglicorum in Latinum et Græcum conversæ. 8vo. Vol. I. 10s. 6d. Vol. II. 12s.

Foliorum Centuriæ. Select Passages for Translation into Latin and Greek Prose. 7th Edition. Post 8vo. 8s.

TRANSLATIONS, SELECTIONS, &c.

** Many of the following books are well adapted for School Prizes.

Æschylus. Translated into English Prose by F. A. Paley, M.A. 2nd Edition. 8vo. 7s. 6d.

—— Translated into English Verse by Anna Swanwick. Post 8vo. 5s.

—— Folio Edition, with 33 Illustrations after Flaxman. 2l. 2s.

Anthologia Græca. A Selection of Choice Greek Poetry, with Notes. By F. St. John Thackeray. 4th and Cheaper Edition. 16mo. 4s. 6d.

Anthologia Latina. A Selection of Choice Latin Poetry, from Nævius to Boëthius, with Notes. By Rev. F. St. John Thackeray. Revised and Cheaper Edition. 16mo. 4s. 6d.

Horace. The Odes and Carmen Sæculare. In English Verse by J. Conington, M.A. 8th edition. Fcap. 8vo. 5s. 6d.

—— The Satires and Epistles. In English Verse by J. Conington, M.A. 5th edition. 6s. 6d.

—— Illustrated from Antique Gems by C. W. King, M.A. The text revised with Introduction by H. A. J. Munro, M.A. Large 8vo. 1l. 1s.

Horace's Odes. Englished and Imitated by various hands. Edited by C. W. F. Cooper. Crown 8vo. 6s. 6d.

Mvsæ Etonenses, sive Carminvm Etonæ Conditorvm Delectvs. By Richard Okes. 2 vols. 8vo. 15s.

Propertius. Verse translations from Book V., with revised Latin Text. By F. A. Paley, M.A. Fcap. 8vo. 3s.

Plato. Gorgias. Translated by E. M. Cope, M.A. 8vo. 7s.

—— Philebus. Translated by F. A. Paley, M.A. Small 8vo. 4s.

—— Theætetus. Translated by F. A. Paley, M.A. Small 8vo, 4s.

—— Analysis and Index of the Dialogues. By Dr. Day. Post 8vo. 5s.

Reddenda Reddita : Passages from English Poetry, with a Latin Verse Translation. By F. E. Gretton. Crown 8vo. 6s.

Sabrinæ Corolla in hortulis Regiæ Scholæ Salopiensis contexuerunt tres viri floribus legendis. Editio tertia. 8vo. 8s. 6d.

Sertum Carthusianum Floribus trium Seculorum Contextum. By W. H. Brown. 8vo. 14s.

Theocritus. In English Verse, by C. S. Calverley, M.A. Crown 8vo. [*New Edition, Preparing.*

Translations into English and Latin. By C. S. Calverley, M.A. Post 8vo. 7s. 6d.

—— *by* ... ... M A . H Jackson, M.A., and W. E. Currey, M.A. Crown 8vo. 8s.

—— into Greek and Latin Verse. By R. C. Jebb. 4to. cloth gilt. 10s. 6d.

Between Whiles. Translations by B. H. Kennedy. Crown 8vo. 6s.

REFERENCE VOLUMES.

A Latin Grammar. By Albert Harkness. Post 8vo. 6s.

—————— By T. H. Key, M.A. 6th Thousand. Post 8vo. 8s.

A Short Latin Grammar for Schools. By T. H. Key, M.A., F.R.S. 14th Edition. Post 8vo. 3s. 6d.

A Guide to the Choice of Classical Books. By J. B. Mayor, M.A. Revised Edition. Crown 8vo. 3s.

The Theatre of the Greeks. By J. W. Donaldson, D.D. 8th Edition. Post 8vo. 5s.

Keightley's Mythology of Greece and Italy. 4th Edition. 5s.

A Dictionary of Latin and Greek Quotations. By H. T. Riley. Post 8vo. 5s. With Index Verborum, 6s.

A History of Roman Literature. By W. S. Teuffel, Professor at the University of Tübingen. By W. Wagner, Ph.D. 2 vols. Demy 8vo. 21s.

Student's Guide to the University of Cambridge. 4th Edition revised. Fcap. 8vo. Part 1, 2s. 6d.; Parts 2 to 6, 1s. each.

CLASSICAL TABLES.

Latin Accidence. By the Rev. P. Frost, M.A. 1s.

Latin Versification. 1s.

Notabilia Quaedam; or the Principal Tenses of most of the Irregular Greek Verbs and Elementary Greek, Latin, and French Construction. New edition. 1s.

Richmond Rules for the Ovidian Distich, &c. By J. Tate, M.A. 1s.

The Principles of Latin Syntax. 1s.

Greek Verbs. A Catalogue of Verbs, Irregular and Defective; their leading formations, tenses, and inflexions, with Paradigms for conjugation, Rules for formation of tenses, &c. &c. By J. S. Baird, T.C.D. 2s. 6d.

Greek Accents (Notes on). By A. Barry, D.D. New Edition. 1s.

Homeric Dialect. Its Leading Forms and Peculiarities. By J. S. Baird, T.C.D. New edition, by W. G. Rutherford. 1s.

Greek Accidence. By the Rev. P. Frost, M.A. New Edition. 1s.

CAMBRIDGE MATHEMATICAL SERIES.

Whitworth's Choice and Chance. 3rd Edition. Crown 8vo. 6s.

McDowell's Exercises on Euclid and in Modern Geometry. 3rd Edition. 6s.

Vyvyan's Trigonometry. Sewed.

Taylor's Geometry of Conics. Elementary. 3rd Edition 4s. 6d.

—————— ——— ——— ———— y. 3rd Edition. 6s.

Garnett's Elementary Dynamics. 2nd Edition. 6s.

—————— Heat, an Elementary Treatise. 2nd Edition. 3s. 6d.

Walton's Elementary Mechanics (Problems in). 2nd Edition. 6s.

CAMBRIDGE SCHOOL AND COLLEGE TEXT-BOOKS.

A Series of Elementary Treatises for the use of Students in the Universities, Schools, and Candidates for the Public Examinations. Fcap. 8vo.

Arithmetic. By Rev. C. Elsee, M.A. Fcap. 8vo. 10th Edit. 3s. 6d.

Algebra. By the Rev. C. Elsee, M.A. 6th Edit. 4s.

Arithmetic. By A. Wrigley, M.A. 3s. 6d.

—— A Progressive Course of Examples. With Answers. By J. Watson, M.A. 5th Edition. 2s. 6d.

Algebra. Progressive Course of Examples. By Rev. W. F. M'Michael, M.A., and R. Prowde Smith, M.A. 2nd Edition. 3s. 6d. With Answers. 4s. 6d.

Plane Astronomy, An Introduction to. By P. T. Main, M.A. 4th Edition. 4s.

Conic Sections treated Geometrically. By W. H. Besant, M.A. 4th Edition. 4s. 6d.

Elementary Conic Sections treated Geometrically. By W. H. Besant, M.A. [*In the Press.*

Statics, Elementary. By Rev. H. Goodwin, D.D. 2nd Edit. 3s.

Hydrostatics, Elementary. By W. H. Besant, M.A. 10th Edit. 4s.

Mensuration, An Elementary Treatise on. By B. T. Moore, M.A. 6s.

Newton's Principia, The First Three Sections of, with an Appendix; and the Ninth and Eleventh Sections. By J. H. Evans, M.A. 5th Edition, by P. T. Main, M.A. 4s.

Trigonometry, Elementary. By T. P. Hudson, M.A. 3s. 6d.

Optics, Geometrical. With Answers. By W. S. Aldis, M.A. 3s. 6d.

Analytical Geometry for Schools. By T. G. Vyvyan. 3rd Edit. 4s. 6d.

Greek Testament, Companion to the. By A. C. Barrett, A.M. 4th Edition, revised. Fcap. 8vo. 5s.

Book of Common Prayer, An Historical and Explanatory Treatise on the. By W. G. Humphry, B.D. 6th Edition. Fcap. 8vo. 4s. 6d.

Music, Text-book of. By H. C. Banister. 9th Edit. revised. 5s.

—— Concise History of. By Rev. H. G. Bonavia Hunt, B. Mus. Oxon. 5th Edition revised. 3s. 6d.

ARITHMETIC AND ALGEBRA.
See foregoing Series.

GEOMETRY AND EUCLID.

Text-Book of Geometry. By T. S. Aldis, M.A. Small 8vo. 4s. 6d. Part I. 2s. 6d. Part II. 2s.

The Elements of Euclid. By H. J. Hose. Fcap. 8vo. 4s. 6d. Exercises separately, 1s.

—— The First Six Books, with Commentary by Dr. Lardner. 10th Edition. 8vo. 6s.

—— The First Two Books explained to Beginners. By C. P. Mason, B.A. 2nd Edition. Fcap 8vo. 2s. 6d.

The Enunciations and Figures to Euclid's Elements. By Rev. J. Brasse, D.D. New Edition. Fcap. 8vo. 1s. On Cards, in case, 5s. 6d. Without the Figures, 6d.

Exercises on Euclid and in Modern Geometry. By J. McDowell, B.A. Crown 8vo. 3rd Edition revised. 6s.

Geometrical Conic Sections. By W. H. Besant, M.A. 4th Edit. 1s. 6d.

Elementary Geometrical Conic Sections. By W. H. Besant, M.A. [*In the Press.*

Elementary Geometry of Conics. By C. Taylor, M.A. 3rd Edit. 8vo. 4s. 6d.

An Introduction to Ancient and Modern Geometry of Conics. By C. Taylor, M.A. 8vo. 15s.

Solutions of Geometrical Problems, proposed at St. John's College from 1830 to 1846. By T. Gaskin, M.A. 8vo. 12s.

TRIGONOMETRY.

Trigonometry. Introduction to Plane. By Rev. T. G. Vyvyan, Charterhouse. Cr. 8vo. Sewed.

Elementary Trigonometry. By T. P. Hudson, M.A. 3s. 6d.

An Elementary Treatise on Mensuration. By B. T. Moore, M.A. 5s.

ANALYTICAL GEOMETRY
AND DIFFERENTIAL CALCULUS.

An Introduction to Analytical Plane Geometry. By W. P. Turnbull, M.A. 8vo. 12s.

Problems on the Principles of Plane Co-ordinate Geometry. By W. Walton, M.A. 8vo. 16s.

Trilinear Co-ordinates, and Modern Analytical Geometry of Two Dimensions. By W. A. Whitworth, M.A. 8vo. 16s.

An Elementary Treatise on Solid Geometry. By W. S. Aldis, M.A. 2nd Edition revised. 8vo. 8s.

Elementary Treatise on the Differential Calculus. By M. O'Brien, M.A. 8vo. 10s. 6d.

Elliptic Functions, Elementary Treatise on. By A. Cayley, M.A. Demy 8vo. 15s.

MECHANICS & NATURAL PHILOSOPHY.

Statics, Elementary. By H. Goodwin, D.D. Fcap. 8vo. 2nd Edition. 3s.

Dynamics, A Treatise on Elementary. By W. Garnett, M.A. 2nd Edition. Crown 8vo. 6s.

Elementary Mechanics, Problems in. By W. Walton, M.A. New Edition. Crown 8vo. 6s.

Theoretical Mechanics, Problems in. By W. Walton. 2nd Edit. revised and enlarged. Demy 8vo. 16s.

Hydrostatics. By W. H. Besant, M.A. Fcap. 8vo. 10th Edition. 4s.

Hydromechanics, A Treatise on. By W. H. Besant, M.A. 8vo. New Edition revised. 10s. 6d.

Dynamics of a Particle, A Treatise on the. By W. H. Besant, M.A. [*Preparing.*

Optics, Geometrical. By W. S. Aldis, M.A. Fcap. 8vo. 3s. 6d.

Double Refraction, A Chapter on Fresnel's Theory of. By W. S. Aldis, M.A. 8vo. 2s.

Heat, An Elementary Treatise on. By W. Garnett, M.A. Crown 8vo. 2nd Edition revised. 3s. 6d.

Newton's Principia, The First Three Sections of, with an Appendix; and the Ninth and Eleventh Sections. By J. H. Evans, M.A. 5th Edition. Edited by P. T. Main, M.A. 4s.

Astronomy, An Introduction to Plane. By P. T. Main, M.A. Fcap. 8vo. cloth. 4s.

Astronomy, Practical and Spherical. By R. Main, M.A. 8vo. 14s.

Astronomy, Elementary Chapters on, from the 'Astronomie Physique' of Biot. By H. Goodwin, D.D. 8vo. 3s. 6d.

Pure Mathematics and Natural Philosophy, A Compendium of Facts and Formulæ in. By G. R. Smalley. Fcap. 8vo. 3s. 6d.

Elementary Course of Mathematics. By H. Goodwin, D.D. 6th Edition. 8vo. 16s.

Problems and Examples, adapted to the 'Elementary Course of Mathematics.' 3rd Edition. 8vo. 5s.

Solutions of Goodwin's Collection of Problems and Examples. By W. W. Hutt, M.A. 3rd Edition, revised and enlarged. 8vo. 9s.

Pure Mathematics, Elementary Examples in. By J. Taylor. 8vo. 7s. 6d.

Mechanics of Construction. With numerous Examples. By S. Fenwick, F.R.A.S. 8vo. 12s.

Pure and Applied Calculation, Notes on the Principles of. By Rev. J. Challis, M.A. Demy 8vo. 15s.

Physics, The Mathematical Principle of. By Rev. J. Challis, M A. Demy 8vo. 5s.

TECHNOLOGICAL HANDBOOKS.

Edited by H. TRUEMAN WOOD, Secretary of the Society of Arts.

1. Dyeing and Tissue Printing. By W. Crookes, F.R.S. [*In the press.*

2. Iron and Steel. By Prof. A. K. Huntington, of King's College. [*Preparing.*

3. Cotton Manufacture. By Richard Marsden, Esq., of Manchester. [*Preparing.*

4. Telegraphs and Telephones. By W. H. Preece, F.R.S. [*Preparing.*

5. Glass Manufacture. By Henry Chance, M.A.; H. Powell, B.A.; and John Hopkinson, M.A., LL.D., F.R.S.

HISTORY, TOPOGRAPHY, &c.

Rome and the Campagna. By R. Burn, M.A. With 85 Engravings and 26 Maps and Plans. With Appendix. 4to. 3*l.* 3*s.*

Old Rome. A Handbook for Travellers. By R. Burn, M.A. With Maps and Plans. Demy 8vo. 10*s.* 6*l.*

Modern Europe. By Dr. T. H. Dyer. 2nd Edition, revised and continued. 5 vols. Demy 8vo. 2*l.* 12*s.* 6*d.*

The History of the Kings of Rome. By Dr. T. H. Dyer. 8vo. 16*s.*

The History of Pompeii: its Buildings and Antiquities. By T. H. Dyer. 3rd Edition, brought down to 1874. Post 8vo. 7*s.* 6*d.*

Ancient Athens: its History, Topography, and Remains. By T. H. Dyer. Super-royal 8vo. Cloth. 1*l.* 5*s.*

The Decline of the Roman Republic. By G. Long. 5 vols. 8vo. 14*s.* each.

A History of England during the Early and Middle Ages. By C. H. Pearson, M.A. 2nd Edition revised and enlarged. 8vo. Vol. I. 16*s.* Vol. II. 14*s.*

Historical Maps of England. By C. H. Pearson. Folio. 2nd Edition revised. 31*s.* 6*d.*

History of England, 1800–15. By Harriet Martineau, with new and copious Index. 1 vol. 3*s.* 6*d.*

History of the Thirty Years' Peace, 1815–46. By Harriet Martineau. 4 vols. 3*s.* 6*d.* each.

A Practical Synopsis of English History. By A. Bowes. 4th Edition. 8vo. 2*s.*

Student's Text-Book of English and General History. By D. Beale. Crown 8vo. 2*s.* 6*d.*

Lives of the Queens of England. By A. Strickland. Library Edition, 8 vols. 7*s.* 6*d.* each. Cheaper Edition, 6 vols. 5*s.* each. Abridged Edition, 1 vol. 6*s.* 6*d.*

Eginhard's Life of Karl the Great (Charlemagne). Translated with Notes, by W. Glaister, M.A., B.C.L. Crown 8vo. 4*s.* 6*d.*

Outlines of Indian History. By A. W. Hughes. Small post 8vo. 3*s.* 6*d.*

The Elements of General History. By Prof. Tytler. New Edition, brought down to 1874. Small post 8vo. 3*s.* 6*d.*

ATLASES.

An Atlas of Classical Geography. 24 Maps. By W. Hughes and G. Long, M.A. New Edition. Imperial 8vo. 12*s.* 6*d.*

A Grammar-School Atlas of Classical Geography. Ten Maps selected from the above. New Edition. Imperial 8vo. 5*s.*

First Classical Maps. By the Rev. J. Tate, M.A. 3rd Edition. Imperial 8vo. 7*s.* 6*d.*

Standard Library Atlas of Classical Geography. Imp. 8vo. 7*s.* 6*d.*

PHILOLOGY.

WEBSTER'S DICTIONARY OF THE ENGLISH LAN-
GUAGE. With Dr. Mahn's Etymology. 1 vol., 1628 Pages, 3000 Illus-
trations. 21s. With Appendices and 70 additional pages of Illustra
tions, 1919 Pages, 31s. 6d.
'THE BEST PRACTICAL ENGLISH DICTIONARY EXTANT.'—*Quarterly Review*, 1873.
Prospectuses, with specimen pages, post free on application.

New Dictionary of the English Language. Combining Explanation with Etymology, and copiously illustrated by Quotations from the
best Authorities. By Dr. Richardson. New Edition, with a Supplement.
2 vols. 4to. 4l. 14s. 6d.; half russia, 5l. 15s. 6d.; russia, 6l. 12s. Supplement
separately. 4to. 12s.
An 8vo. Edit. without the Quotations, 15s.; half russia, 20s.; russia, 24s.

Supplementary English Glossary. Containing 12,000 words and
meanings occurring in English Literature, not found in any other
Dictionary. By T. L. O. Davies. Demy 8vo. 16s.

Dictionary of Corrupted Words. By Rev. A. S. Palmer. [*In the press.*

Brief History of the English Language. By Prof. James Hadley,
LL.D., Yale College. Fcap. 8vo. 1s.

The Elements of the English Language. By E. Adams, Ph.D.
15th Edition. Post 8vo. 4s. 6d.

Philological Essays. By T. H. Key, M.A., F.R.S. 8vo. 10s. 6d.

Language, its Origin and Development. By T. H. Key, M.A.,
F.R.S. 8vo. 14s.

Synonyms and Antonyms of the English Language. By Archdeacon Smith. 2nd Edition. Post 8vo. 5s.

Synonyms Discriminated. By Archdeacon Smith. Demy 8vo. 16s.

Bible English. By T. L. O. Davies. 5s.

The Queen's English. A Manual of Idiom and Usage. By the
late Dean Alford. 5th Edition. Fcap. 8vo. 5s.

Etymological Glossary of nearly 2500 English Words de-
rived from the Greek. By the Rev. E. J. Boyce. Fcap. 8vo. 3s. 6d.

A Syriac Grammar. By G. Phillips, D.D. 3rd Edition, enlarged.
8vo. 7s. 6d.

A Grammar of the Arabic Language. By Rev. W. J. Beau-
mont, M.A. 12mo. 7s.

DIVINITY, MORAL PHILOSOPHY, &c.

Novum Testamentum Græcum, Textus Stephanici, 1550. By
F. H. Scrivener, A.M., LL.D. New Edition. 16mo. 4s. 6d. Also on
Writing Paper, with Wide Margin. Half-bound. 12s.

By the same Author.

Codex Bezæ Cantabrigiensis. 4to. 26s.

A Full Collation of the Codex Sinaiticus with the Received Text
of the New Testament, with Critical Introduction. 2nd Edition, revised.
Fcap. 8vo. 5s.

A Plain Introduction to the Criticism of the New Testament.
With Forty Facsimiles from Ancient Manuscripts. 2nd Edition. 8vo. 16s.

Six Lectures on the Text of the New Testament. For English
Readers. Crown 8vo. 6s.

The New Testament for English Readers. By the late H. Alford, D.D. Vol. I. Part I. 3rd Edit. 12s. Vol. I. Part II. 2nd Edit. 10s. 6d. Vol. II. Part I. 2nd Edit. 16s. Vol. II. Part II. 2nd Edit. 16s.

The Greek Testament. By the late H. Alford, D.D. Vol. I. 6th Edit. 1l. 8s. Vol. II. 6th Edit. 1l. 4s. Vol. III. 5th Edit. 18s. Vol. IV. Part I. 4th Edit. 18s. Vol. IV. Part II. 4th Edit. 14s. Vol. IV. 1l. 12s.

Companion to the Greek Testament. By A. C. Barrett, M.A. 4th Edition, revised. Fcap. 8vo. 5s.

The Book of Psalms. A New Translation, with Introductions, &c. By the Very Rev. J. J. Stewart Perowne, D.D. 8vo. Vol. I. 4th Edition, 18s. Vol. II. 4th Edit. 16s.

—— Abridged for Schools. 3rd Edition. Crown 8vo. 10s. 6d.

History of the Articles of Religion. By C. H. Hardwick. 3rd Edition. Post 8vo. 5s.

History of the Creeds. By J. R. Lumby, D.D. 2nd Edition. Crown 8vo. 7s. 6d.

Pearson on the Creed. Carefully printed from an early edition. With Analysis and Index by E. Walford, M.A. Post 8vo. 5s.

An Historical and Explanatory Treatise on the Book of Common Prayer. By Rev. W. G. Humphry, B.D. 6th Edition, enlarged. Small post 8vo. 4s. 6d.

The New Table of Lessons Explained. By Rev. W. G. Humphry, B.D. Fcap. 1s. 6d.

A Commentary on the Gospels for the Sundays and other Holy Days of the Christian Year. By Rev. W. Denton, A.M. New Edition. 3 vols. 8vo. 54s. Sold separately.

Commentary on the Epistles for the Sundays and other Holy Days of the Christian Year. By Rev. W. Denton, A.M. 2 vols. 36s. Sold separately.

Commentary on the Acts. By Rev. W. Denton, A.M. Vol. I. 8vo. 18s. Vol. II. 14s.

Notes on the Catechism. By Rev. A. Barry, D.D. 6th Edit. Fcap. 2s.

Catechetical Hints and Helps. By Rev. E. J. Boyce, M.A. 4th Edition, revised. Fcap. 2s. 6d.

Examination Papers on Religious Instruction. By Rev. E. J. Boyce. Sewed. 1s. 6d.

Church Teaching for the Church's Children. An Exposition of the Catechism. By the Rev. F. W. Harper. Sq. fcap. 2s.

The Winton Church Catechist. Questions and Answers on the Teaching of the Church Catechism. By the late Rev. J. S. B. Monsell, LL.D. 3rd Edition. Cloth, 3s.; or in Four Parts, sewed.

The Church Teacher's Manual of Christian Instruction. By Rev. M. F. Sadler. 21st Thousand. 2s. 6d.

Short Explanation of the Epistles and Gospels of the Chris- tian Year, with Questions. Royal 32mo. 2s. 6d.; calf, 4s. 6d.

Butler's Analogy of Religion; with Introduction and Index by Rev. Dr. Steere. New Edition. Fcap. 3s. 6d.

—— **Three Sermons on Human Nature, and Dissertation on** Virtue. By W. Whewell, D.D. 4th Edition. Fcap. 8vo. 2s. 6d.

Lectures on the History of Moral Philosophy in England. By W. Whewell, D.D. Crown 8vo. 8s.

Kent's Commentary on International Law. By J. T. Abdy, LL.D. New and Cheap Edition. Crown 8vo. 10s. 6d.

A Manual of the Roman Civil Law. By G. Leapingwell, LL.D. 8vo. 12s.

FOREIGN CLASSICS.

A series for use in Schools, with English Notes, grammatical and explanatory, and renderings of difficult idiomatic expressions.
Fcap. 8vo.

Schiller's Wallenstein. By Dr. A. Buchheim. 3rd Edit. 6s. 6d. Or the Lager and Piccolomini, 3s. 6d. Wallenstein's Tod, 3s. 6d.

—— Maid of Orleans. By Dr. W. Wagner. 3s. 6d.

—— Maria Stuart. By V. Kastner. 3s.

Goethe's Hermann and Dorothea. By E. Bell, M.A., and E. Wölfel. 2s. 6d.

German Ballads, from Uhland, Goethe, and Schiller. By C. L. Bielefeld. 3rd Edition. 3s. 6d.

Charles XII., par Voltaire. By L. Direy. 4th Edition. 3s. 6d.

Aventures de Télémaque, par Fénélon. By C. J. Delille. 2nd Edition. 4s. 6d.

Select Fables of La Fontaine. By F. E. A. Gasc. 14th Edition. 3s.

Picciola, by X. B. Saintine. By Dr. Dubuc. 11th Thousand. 3s. 6d.

FRENCH CLASS-BOOKS.

Twenty Lessons in French. With Vocabulary, giving the Pronunciation. By W. Brebner. Post 8vo. 4s.

French Grammar for Public Schools. By Rev. A. C. Clapin, M.A. Fcap. 8vo. 8th Edit. 2s. 6d.

French Primer. By Rev. A. C. Clapin, M.A. Fcap. 8vo. 4th Edit. 1s.

Primer of French Philology. By Rev. A. C. Clapin. Fcap. 8vo. 1s.

Le Nouveau Trésor; or, French Student's Companion. By M. E. S. 16th Edition. Fcap. 8vo. 3s. 6d.

F. E. A. GASC'S FRENCH COURSE.

First French Book. Fcap 8vo. 76th Thousand. 1s. 6d.

Second French Book. 37th Thousand. Fcap. 8vo. 2s. 6d.

Key to First and Second French Books. Fcap. 8vo. 3s. 6d.

French Fables for Beginners, in Prose, with Index. 14th Thousand. 12mo. 2s.

Select Fables of La Fontaine. New Edition. Fcap. 8vo. 3s.

Histoires Amusantes et Instructives. With Notes. 14th Thousand. Fcap. 8vo. 2s. 6d.

Practical Guide to Modern French Conversation. 12th Thousand. Fcap. 8vo. 2s. 6d.

French Poetry for the Young. With Notes. 4th Edition. Fcap. 8vo. 2s.

Materials for French Prose Composition; or, Selections from the best English Prose Writers. 15th Thousand. Fcap. 8vo. 4s. 6d. Key, 6s.

Prosateurs Contemporains. With Notes. 8vo. 6th Edition, revised. 5s.

Le Petit Compagnon; a French Talk-Book for Little Children. 10th Thousand. 16mo. 2s. 6d.

An Improved Modern Pocket Dictionary of the French and English Languages. 30th Thousand, with Additions. 16mo. Cloth. 4s. Also in 2 vols., in neat leatherette, 5s.

Modern French-English and English-French Dictionary. 2nd Edition, revised. In 1 vol. 12s. 6d. (formerly 2 vols. 25s.)

GOMBERT'S FRENCH DRAMA.

Being a Selection of the best Tragedies and Comedies of Molière, Racine, Corneille, and Voltaire. With Arguments and Notes by A. Gombert. New Edition, revised by F. E. A. Gasc. Fcap. 8vo. 1s. each; sewed, 6d.   CONTENTS.

MOLIERE:—Le Misanthrope. L'Avare. Le Bourgeois Gentilhomme. Le Tartuffe. Le Malade Imaginaire. Les Femmes Savantes. Les Fourberies de Scapin. Les Précieuses Ridicules. L'Ecole des Femmes. L'Ecole des Maris. Le Médecin malgré Lui.

RACINE:—Phédre. Esther. Athalie. Iphigénie. Les Plaideurs. La Thébaïde; or, Les Frères Ennemis. Andromaque. Britannicus.

P. CORNEILLE:—Le Cid. Horace. Cinna. Polyeucte.

VOLTAIRE:—Zaïre.

GERMAN CLASS-BOOKS.

Materials for German Prose Composition. By Dr Buchheim. 7th Edition Fcap. 4s. 6d. Key, 3s.

A German Grammar for Public Schools. By the Rev. A. C. Clapin and F. Holl Müller. 2nd Edition. Fcap. 2s. 6d.

Kotzebue's Der Gefangene. With Notes by Dr. W. Stromberg. 1s.

ENGLISH CLASS-BOOKS.

A Brief History of the English Language. By Prof. Jas. Hadley, LL.D., of Yale College. Fcap. 8vo. 1s.

The Elements of the English Language. By E. Adams, Ph.D. 18th Edition. Post 8vo. 4s. 6d.

The Rudiments of English Grammar and Analysis. By E. Adams, Ph.D. 8th Edition. Fcap. 8vo. 2s.

By C. P. MASON, Fellow of Univ. Coll. London.

First Notions of Grammar for Young Learners. Fcap. 8vo. 10th Thousand. Cloth. 8d.

First Steps in English Grammar for Junior Classes. Demy 18mo. New Edition. 1s.

Outlines of English Grammar for the use of Junior Classes.
26th Thousand. Crown 8vo. 2s.

English Grammar, including the Principles of Grammatical
Analysis. 24th Edition. 77th Thousand. Crown 8vo. 3s. 6d.

A Shorter English Grammar, with copious Exercises. 8th Thousand. Crown 8vo. 3s. 6d.

English Grammar Practice, being the Exercises separately. 1s.

Edited for Middle-Class Examinations.

With Notes on the Analysis and Parsing, and Explanatory Remarks.

Milton's Paradise Lost, Book I. With Life. 3rd Edit. Post 8vo.
2s

—— Book II. With Life. 2nd Edit. Post 8vo. 2s.

—— Book III. With Life. Post 8vo. 2s.

Goldsmith's Deserted Village. With Life. Post 8vo. 1s. 6d.

Cowper's Task, Book II. With Life. Post 8vo. 2s.

Thomson's Spring. With Life. Post 8vo. 2s.

—— Winter. With Life. Post 8vo. 2s.

Practical Hints on Teaching. By Rev. J. Menet, M.A. 5th Edit.
Crown 8vo. cloth, 2s. 6d. ; paper, 2s.

Test Lessons in Dictation. 2nd Edition. Paper cover, 1s. 6d.

Questions for Examinations in English Literature. By Rev.
W. W. Skeat, Prof. of Anglo-Saxon at Cambridge University. 2s. 6d.

Drawing Copies. By P. H. Delamotte. Oblong 8vo. 12s. Sold
also in parts at 1s. each.

Poetry for the School-room. New Edition. Fcap. 8vo. 1s. 6d.

Geographical Text-Book; a Practical Geography. By M. E. S.
12mo. 2s.
    The Blank Maps done up separately, 4to. 2s. coloured.

Loudon's (Mrs.) Entertaining Naturalist. New Edition. Revised
by W. S. Dallas, F.L.S. 5s.

—— Handbook of Botany. New Edition, greatly enlarged by
D. Wooster. Fcap. 2s. 6d.

The Botanist's Pocket-Book. With a copious Index. By W. R.
Hayward. 3rd Edit. revised. Crown 8vo. Cloth limp. 4s. 6d.

Experimental Chemistry, founded on the Work of Dr. Stöckhardt.
By C. W. Heaton. Post 8vo. 5s.

Double Entry Elucidated. By B. W. Foster. 12th Edit. 4to.
3s. 6d.

A New Manual of Book-keeping. By P. Crellin, Accountant.
Crown 8vo. 3s. 6d.

Picture School-Books. In Simple Language, with numerous Illustrations. Royal 16mo.

School Primer. 6d.—School Reader. By J. Tilleard. 1s.—Poetry Book for Schools. 1s.—The Life of Joseph. 1s.—The Scripture Parables. By the Rev. J. E. Clarke. 1s.—The Scripture Miracles. By the Rev. J. E. Clarke. 1s.—The New Testament History. By the Rev. J. G. Wood, M.A. 1s.—The Old Testament History. By the Rev. J. G. Wood, M.A. 1s.—The Story of Bunyan's Pilgrim's Progress. 1s.—The Life of Christopher Columbus. By Sarah Crompton. 1s.—The Life of Martin Luther. By Sarah Crompton. 1s.

BOOKS FOR YOUNG READERS.

In 8 vols. Limp cloth, 6d. each.

The Cat and the Hen; Sam and his Dog Red-leg; Bob and Tom Lee; A Wreck——The New-born Lamb; Rosewood Box; Poor Fan; Wise Dog——The Three Monkeys——Story of a Cat, told by Herself——The Blind Boy; The Mute Girl; A New Tale of Babes in a Wood——The Dey and the Knight; The New Bank-note; The Royal Visit; A King's Walk on a Winter's Day——Queen Bee and Busy Bee——Gull's Crag, a Story of the Sea.

First Book of Geography. By C. A. Johns. 1s.

BELL'S READING-BOOKS.

FOR SCHOOLS AND PAROCHIAL LIBRARIES.

The popularity which the 'Books for Young Readers' have attained is a sufficient proof that teachers and pupils alike approve of the use of interesting stories, with a simple plot in place of the dry combination of letters and syllables, making no impression on the mind, of which elementary reading-books generally consist.

The Publishers have therefore thought it advisable to extend the application of this principle to books adapted for more advanced readers.

Now Ready. Post 8vo. Strongly bound.

Masterman Ready. By Captain Marryat, R.N. 1s. 6d.

The Settlers in Canada. By Captain Marryat, R.N. 1s. 6d.

Parables from Nature. (Selected.) By Mrs. Gatty. 1s.

Friends in Fur and Feathers. By Gwynfryn. 1s.

Robinson Crusoe. 1s. 6d.

Andersen's Danish Tales. (Selected.) By E. Bell, M.A. 1s.

Southey's Life of Nelson. (Abridged.) 1s.

Grimm's German Tales. (Selected.) By E. Bell, M.A. 1s.

Life of the Duke of Wellington, with Maps and Plans. 1s.

Marie; or, Glimpses of Life in France. By A. R. Ellis. 1s.

Poetry for Boys. By D. Munro. 1s.

Edgeworth's Tales; a Selection. 1s.

Great Englishmen; Short Lives for Young Children. 1s.

Others in Preparation.

LONDON:

Printed by STRANGEWAYS & SONS, Tower Street, Upper St. Martin's Lane.